We Live
Forever

We Live Forever

THE REAL TRUTH ABOUT DEATH

P.M.H. ATWATER, L.H.D.

ARE
PRESS

ASSOCIATION FOR
RESEARCH AND
ENLIGHTENMENT

A.R.E. Press • Virginia Beach • Virginia

A.R.E. Press
215 67th Street
Virginia Beach, VA 23451-2061

Library of Congress Cataloguing-in-Publication Data
Atwater, P.M.H.
    We live forever : the real truth about death / by P.M.H. Atwater.
        p.   cm.
    Includes bibliographical references.
    ISBN 0-87604-492-5 (trade pbk.)
    1. Near-death experiences. I. Title.
BF1045.N4A88 2004
133.9'01'3—dc22

                                        2004008771

Cover design by Richard Boyle

This book is lovingly dedicated to:

Myriam Renee Huffman
and
Louisa Mae Huffman

My personal experiences have taught me that a partnership exists between life and death, and that death, as a shape-shifter, shepherds the time we have in this world to express ourselves and because of that expression, to grow.

Any "veil" that appears to separate life from death is actually self-created by those who are afraid to recognize and accept the power of their true identity as divine beings of a Higher Order.

Another agenda holds sway to life's beginnings and endings—the will of the soul.

Contents

Introduction

"We are either pulled by a vision, or pushed by pain."
—*Rev. Dr. Michael Beckwith*

The subjects in this book strike at the very core of the human family: who we are, what we're doing here, and where we're headed. This book has been long in the making because, quite frankly, I didn't have the guts to write it before. What changed for me? Well, I got real. I decided to shift my emphasis from thinking like a researcher to feeling like a person. That means, it's time for me to "own" my own experiences, claim them. I've been speaking on behalf of others for twenty-five years as a disciplined, scientific investigator. Now it's my turn to open up and say what I really want to say.

It's only fair, though, that you know something about me to begin with, so, let's get acquainted.

I'm past retirement age, still snappy, lots of energy and drive, and as passionate as ever. My former marriage lasted twenty years; the present one looks like it'll go on forever and I couldn't be happier. I've birthed and raised three children, miscarried three, have four living grandchildren (one more in spirit), was born in Twin Falls, Idaho, and died in Boise. Yes, you heard me right. I'm one of those near-death experiencers who physically died (as near as the medical community can determine), encountered life on "the other side" of death, and revived to tell of it. I did this three times in three months in 1977. It's because of my third episode that I became a researcher of near-death states, but it was Elisabeth Kübler-Ross who got me started.

We huddled together, just the two of us, on a bench at Chicago's O'Hare Airport back in July of 1978. Our nonstop chattering went on for over an hour: me, describing the three times I had died the previous year and what I had experienced each time on "the other side" of death; and she, in recognition of what she had heard, naming my episodes "near-death experiences" and me a "near-death survivor."

In doing this, Elisabeth validated me. She said I wasn't crazy, that what had happened to me was real and I could believe it. There are no words to describe the relief I felt when she said that. Her unquestioned expertise in the field of death and dying, however, did not suffice. I needed to know more. I had questions.

I began asking my questions that November, once I had moved from Boise to the state of Virginia. My research base now totals sessions with over 3,000 adult and 277 child experiencers, plus many of their significant others; six books record my findings; as well as a web site that is filled with even more information.

This effort can be matched with its duplicate: the years between 1966 and 1977 that I spent investigating altered states of consciousness, mysticism, hauntings, paranormal phenomena, and varied forms of spirituality. I launched this earlier work after reading *The Sleeping Prophet* by Jess Stearn—a book about a most unusual psychic by the name of Edgar Cayce. The book changed my life in how it enabled me to view my childhood differently and set me free to explore larger venues without fear or hesitation.

I actually conducted my first double-blind, control-group study at the age of five, though. I was experimenting with mud pies to arrive at the ratio of soil, water, and temperature needed to create the master-piece of color and texture I wanted. I did the same thing when I learned to cook. It drove my mother nuts.

In the personal quotes and sharings this book is packed with, you'll have an opportunity to see how individual experiences—yours and mine—can lead to greater truth. You'll also have an opportunity to know that, far from being a disciplined researcher, I am a very human woman who loves deeply, laughs much, and is intensely curious.

1

Myriam's Gift

"You meet your destiny on the road you take to avoid it."
—Carl Gustav Jung

The unthinkable happened.

Myriam, an incredibly lively, beautiful, curious two-year-old with a decided mind of her own was rushed to the hospital on Thursday, December 16, 1999, pronounced brain dead the following afternoon, and died that evening. We learned later that her brain had collapsed onto her brain stem. Bacterial meningitis.

By the time my youngest daughter, Paulie, and I could fly to San Jose, California, from Virginia, the faces of Kelly and Lydia, Myriam's parents, were shrouded in a pasty blankness—that death mask people wear who have suffered a grievous loss. Like robots, they shuffled through the demands of their fledgling business. They had workers on job sites. Deadlines pressed. The phone rang incessantly.

A crush of aunts and uncles, grandparents and friends, gathered in the tiny house to do what they could to help. Aaron, two

∞

years older than his sister, Myriam, gaped in awe at all the touching, sharing, crying, and hugging that happened as photos of happier times passed from hand to hand and memories found voices. Grief. Sobs. Laughter. Pain.

A family in crisis—my son and firstborn, my daughter-in-law, her kin, ours.

So, in the name of love, the crowd of us tripped over each other's feet in an inexplicable urge to "do something." Food was cooked, although few had an appetite. Errands were run, even though those who knew the way got lost running them. Clutches formed around the I-can't-stand-it-any-longer smokers, the pink-skinned fresh-air freaks, the nonstop chatterboxes, the God-love-'em clean team, and the kid pals who spent their time frolicking on the floor with Aaron. Those who claimed the right to grieve alone still wandered in and out the front door as if drawn to the warmth of noisy bodies and the sounds and smells of humanness.

Comments lingered in the air, waiting to be repeated to each new visitor.

Kelly remembered that: "Towards the end, the feelings between Myriam and I were much stronger. She really appreciated being with Daddy. This was new, as Mommy had always come first before. I wish she were here right now. I miss her terribly."

Lydia spoke of rushing her daughter to the emergency room at O'Connor Hospital in Santa Clara. "They got her on antiseizure medica-tion, called a pediatrics specialist, and sent her to San Jose Medical Cen-ter with the specialist at her side. Kelly met me at the intensive care unit after he had telephoned his sister Natalie to come take care of Aaron. She was right there. From that moment on, Kelly and I knew Myriam's time on earth was over. We spent the whole night crying and consoling each other."

Diane, Lydia's mom, struggled with the specter of blame. "When I told Kathi, the doctor I work for, that Myriam's brain had herniated into her brain stem sometime after they did a spinal tap, she responded that this was a risk with spinal taps. I have dark thoughts about that and felt the doctors made a horrible mistake, that perhaps Myriam would be here if they hadn't done that. I was sobbing, inconsolable. Kathi held me in her arms, trying to comfort me, and said, 'Don't even go there. The doctors had to do what they did.'"

John, Kelly's father, grimaced. "I felt hurt when I heard the news. Deep! You're so helpless. My granddaughter is dead. I was here with my wife, Anne, a little over a month ago to celebrate our birthdays. Myriam was two and I was seventy, sixty-eight years' difference to the day between our ages."

So it went, with each person taking turns weaving emotion into a single tapestry of sound-threads.

Our family, once we were notified of the impending crisis, called every prayer group we could locate. Thousands of people responded. In less than a heartbeat, the oneness of family grew to embrace loving, caring people throughout the entire nation. Affiliations or religious beliefs were never questioned. All that mattered was the life of this precious child. We prayed for a miracle, refusing to think a single negative thought. But the miracle never happened.

A senseless tragedy?

Yes, it was. Yet there is far more to Myriam's death than the pain of her sudden passing. Most of us received intuitive warnings in advance about what was coming. There were spirit visitations and past-life connections and otherworldly revelations that centered around a larger-than-life truth: *Death ends nothing but the physical body.*

This challenged us to embrace a greater vision of what we thought we knew. It stretched our family, bringing us to the point where we came to realize that through the simple acts of being born and dying, we each, as "givers of gifts," enrich all that life is. We give the gift of our potential at birth, what we can become. At death, we leave the gift of our achievement, what we did with what we had.

Two gifts: one we bring in with us; one we leave behind after we're gone. Whether coming or going, we bless this world with the gifts that our existence bestows.

Myriam's potential from the moment of her birth was as bright and beautiful as she was. There's no doubting that. But what she left us with, well, that caught everyone off guard, including me. Myriam's gift, the sum of what she had to offer, was uncompromising honesty. Never could she tolerate pretense, denials, anything hidden, anything avoided. It was as if she possessed X-ray vision and could see right through you— as if the sole purpose of her brief stay on earth was to insist that those who were touched by her life should release whatever it was that held them back from recognizing and expressing the fullness of their true authentic self. No excuses. No exceptions.

The repercussions of Myriam's gift were as startling as the probe of her gaze.

In our family, Kelly and Lydia admitted their marriage was miscast from its inception, and they divorced. Natalie, possessed of new courage and faith, stepped forward into marriage and motherhood, and found a happiness never known to her before. Paulie confronted her past and uncovered the reason behind her many heartbreaks. John returned to his home in Washington more appreciative of the life he and Anne enjoyed, and he rededicated himself to helping others, especially immigrants to this country from war-weary nations. Diane grew wiser as her focus shifted to the deeper reaches of strength and vision within her. There were others, additional relatives and friends, whose lives were transformed as well.

And me?

My change came when the full impact of Myriam's insistence on complete and utter honesty demanded that I face what I had been side-stepping for years: taking a personal stand on what death had taught me; in essence, owning my own truth.

You see, for a quarter of a century, I have devoted myself entirely to researching near-death experiences. I have said no to most of the invitations I have received for rest and recreation, turned away from opportunities that might have led to careers I would have preferred, and immersed myself instead in the rigor of objective observation and analysis. For the most part, the three near-death episodes I had in 1977 and how the aftereffects affected me were stored away on the back shelf of my mind, used only in brief as examples in the six books I wrote about my findings. What mattered, all that mattered, was what I could substantiate from the thousands of experiencers with whom I had had sessions. Allowing myself to be too personal would have biased my research. My job, as I saw it, was to become a blank slate on which others could "write" their story.

I do not regret the sacrifices I made in this pursuit or what I went through to produce the books I have written. But Myriam stopped me short. She flung wide the doors of my heart and validated the songs my soul sings.

Thanks to the gift of Myriam's life, what made her special, I can now share the gift of my many moments at the edge of death and beyond. Strange as it may seem, however, death has been my teacher for a long time—since I was a child.

2

Gold Stars, Windshields, and Keyholes

"Nothing in life is to be feared, only understood."
—Madame Marie Curie

I walked the path of death as a youngster, and it terrified me so much that it imprinted all the years that followed. Knowing about what happened then, as well as a few other incidents that occurred later on, will help you to understand why death came to overshadow my life.

Pearl Harbor. Two words that even now bring back vivid memories of people screaming and crying, in the house where I lived and outside on the streets. It's as though the bombs were dropped in our own neighborhood; that's the impact that one event had on my world.

Rationing, air raid drills, collecting metal, and victory gardens were the order of the day. Grocery stores had sparsely filled shelves

7

but boasted large tables and vats at the ready in case you had enough produce from your garden to can. Along with paying for the items you wanted to purchase at the checkout stand, you also paid for any tin you used in canning. My mother and I sometimes walked to the local library where, in the basement, women gathered to roll bandages for the troops. My job was making Q-Tips. I wasn't very good at it.

Every morning I passed signs of death on my way to school. At that time if anyone in your family died in the war effort, you placed a large decal of a gold star in your living-room window. I knew what those gold stars meant. Once I passed a house where six new gold stars had been added overnight. I just stood there sobbing. I do not recall a single morning in my entire first-grade experience that wasn't spent quieting my sobs and shudders and feigning bravery as I walked into my classroom.

After that, I could never understand why teachers used gold stars to reward good behavior or a job well done. To me, gold stars were a symbol of death and horror and loved ones who never came home to their families. Because of this association, I grew up avoiding anything that might entitle me to a reward. I didn't make peace with gold until I was in my late fifties; I couldn't even wear the stuff until I turned sixty.

I was in the third grade when my mother finally found the right man and settled down. Our house was near the lip of Rock Creek Canyon, south of Twin Falls. Mostly we raised, canned, or froze our own food, including meat. My job was the chicken coop; I gathered eggs and removed the carcass of any hen who died overnight. I'd go screaming into the house, completely undone at the trauma of picking up a dead chicken, only to have its guts spew out in a flood of maggot-thick fluid. Mother would say, "Clean it up. That's your job." We lost a lot of chickens and other animals, too. I grew tired of screaming about this, no one paid much attention to me anyway, so I decided to learn everything I could about life's specter. It wasn't long before I found myself sitting, front row and center, in the most incredible classroom imaginable: my second home, the police station. My mother had married a police officer.

I spent many hours waiting around inside the police station for my new father to take a coffee break so that I could hop a ride home in the squad car. If a call came through while I was with him, I'd have to go along, too, and with strict orders for my behavior: "Don't move, keep your mouth shut, and never tell anyone what you see." I pretty much did what I was told, except for one time when I passed on some information to a cousin who blabbed the story all over the school. Needless to say, I never again mentioned police business after that.

When I was young, television hadn't been invented, so my view screen on the verities and extremes of life was the squad car windshield. I saw a lot, from the more basic scenes of ongoing investigations to the complexities of muggings, attempted murders, beatings, animals run amuck, drunken parties, and the like. Especially during night calls, I'd be utterly transfixed. Since my role was to be invisible, I became the consummate observer, soaking in everything: how people used their bodies, what they said, their expressions, interactions among people, specific movements and what resulted from them.

This early exposure fed my insatiable curiosity. Sometimes during long waits I'd even sneak a peek through the keyhole of the interrogation room. When that wasn't enough, I'd stick my ear to the keyhole. Repeatedly I heard victims telling detectives things like: "I just knew if I turned that corner something awful would happen to me"; or "I had a feeling not to trust that guy." Premonitions, dreams, feelings, almost everyone knew in advance what might happen to him or her if one did this or that. And that puzzled me. Why, I wondered, did people go ahead and do the things they already knew would harm them? Eventually I concluded that all adults were stupid and I never wanted to become one when I grew up.

Such notions were drilled out of my head by my father who had a peculiar way of raising me. We'd go shopping in the five-and-dime stores on Main Street (either Newberry's or Woolworth's) and I, like any kid, would be agog at all the glitter. In those days, most of the counter space was single level and covered with glass. Stacked shelving, what there was of it, was located in the back of the store. The "M.O." (mode of operation) was always the same. Dad would grab me by the shoulders, twirl me around, look at me straight in the eyes, and ask about a passerby: "What was the color of the hair, was it parted, any glasses, describe the face, how about the clothes, any belt, purse, how about the shoes, socks, any wristwatch, what else can you tell me?" We'd cross the inter-section of Main and Shoshone Streets, and Dad would do it again. Same checklist. This continued off and on for three years. I got to the point where I was always staring, never knowing when I would be tested again. Decades later Dad claimed it was all a game. Well, it wasn't a game to me. I swear the man was trying to raise the world's most per-fect witness.

As you can see, the groundwork was laid early on for me to launch search-and-investigative missions just for my own edification. Adults insisted on silent obedience, but I wanted to know things, so I reached out and probed, examined, studied, and experienced. The more I did this, the further away from "the established order" I moved and the closer I came to uncovering what haunted me as a child.

3

We Know When We're Going to Die

"Life is a blackboard upon which we consciously or unconsciously write those messages which govern us. We hold the chalk and the eraser in our mind."—*Ernest Holmes*

Marriage only heightened my curiosity. I was always experimenting. I found that jars sealed better in the pressure cooker if I gave the lids a hot water bath before applying them to the glass lip and screwing on the band. Cakes stayed fresh twice as long if you beat the egg whites to an easy froth and then folded them into the batter. Bulk-pack fruit and vegetables were interchangeable in any recipe: you could substitute pumpkin for applesauce, or use mashed prunes or cooked carrots, squash, peaches, or just about anything you wanted. It didn't matter if you were baking a cake, cookies, or pie, the only limit to what you created was your imagination. Thus, meals at our house were always a surprise.

And so was death.

During the days when my former husband, John, and I leased 160 acres near Filer, there were many farm tragedies. We were privy to all of them. This situation intensified once he became a crop–duster pilot. He specialized in flying night jobs barely inches above the soil of tree–lined farm fields. A number of gruesome and horrible accidents snuffed out innocent lives. We both stared death in the face at moments of personal risk because of auto accidents and serious illness, as did our loved ones and each of our three children. This kind of thing happened so often that for a time I used to set a place for "death" at the kitchen table, replete with dishes and chair, so that our children wouldn't be frightened of our family's familiar consort.

Among what caught my attention then was the incredible number of people who, far from having a brief hunch or scary feeling, actually exhibited preknowledge of their coming death. Conversations my husband and I had with survivors and next of kin revealed intriguing stories about how the deceased must have known what was coming because of the way he or she behaved before the tragedy occurred, shifting routines about three to six months before his or her death.

After a while, I noticed that these changes centered around a need to wrap up business and personal affairs as if there existed some unspoken reason for expediency. Insurance policies took on importance, as did the need to visit loved ones and to be more intimate or philosophical than usual. One last "fling" was often enjoyed before the individual relaxed and was at peace. Just before the death event, the victim seemed to "glow" as if something important were about to happen, something for which the individual had prepared.

Sometimes this preknowledge consisted of more than a series of behavior changes; it was verbal and up front. One such example is the case of a woman in her late twenties who was killed in an early morning automobile pileup on the highway outside Jackpot, Nevada. During the investigation that followed, relatives told the same story—that the woman knew she was going to die, even how and when. She had had a recurring dream starting about six months before, a dream that accurately depicted her death. Because of the dream, she had been getting her life in order and telling others what to expect. No one believed her. After the accident, her loved ones and friends were grief stricken, even more so because of their refusal to give her the benefit of the doubt while she was still alive.

Another incident involved a high school senior who calmly told her parents she would die in a violent accident the day before graduation. This news was given nearly a year in advance, and the announcement sent her parents into a near-frenzy of worry until they convinced themselves that their daughter must be mentally unbalanced. She was sent to several psychologists for evaluation. Each released her with the caution, "Make certain she takes this drug as it will relax her." There was no dream, no reason for the daughter to say such a thing. "I just know," she'd insist, as she readied herself to die.

A year later, and the day before graduation, she and a girlfriend were sitting in a car waiting at an intersection for the light to change when another car suddenly careened out of control and slammed head-on into theirs, killing both girls instantly, yet injuring no one else. Investigators discovered a note the daughter wrote revealing that she knew that she and her best friend would be killed at the same time in the same accident. They also discovered that the other girl had displayed behavioral changes suggestive of someone who knew death was coming, even though she had said nothing to anyone about it.

After another year rolled by, each of the two mothers had a dream in which her deceased daughter returned for a "visit" to explain why she had died. This visitation was so vivid that neither mother could keep it to herself. One of them confided in a local astrologer; very soon the other mother did the same thing. The astrologer contacted the psychologist of the first mother, the one most burdened with grief, for advice on how to handle the situation. I was consulted as well.

A meeting was arranged where all four parents and the psychologist could hear each mother describe her dream. Neither set of parents knew the other before the meeting. Still, the daughters visited their mothers on the same night at about the same time with the same explanation. Both girls had agreed before birth to participate in the violent death event in order that the first one could help the other work through a

∞

lingering fear of dying violently. This death scenario was the only reason each girl gave for having been born. A dramatic healing resulted
from this session, and much pain and grief were released.

Some of our friends were not only agricultural pilots but also corpo-
rate, highway, and construction pilots, as well as flight instructors. A
number of them died in fiery crashes. One such crash took the lives of
two of our best friends when the DeHavilon twin jet they were flying
nose dived into the mesa outside of Boise. It was a stormy night, yet
they canceled their instrument approach, thinking the lights of the city
meant they were closer to the airport than they actually were. Relatives
confirmed that each pilot had exhibited the foreknowledge pattern before the accident as if the event were somehow "expected."

Another crash I was privy to involved a midair collision at midnight
over a farmhouse near Adrian, Oregon. Both pilots plus the farmer's
wife in the house below were killed. The woman was trapped inside
when burning wreckage fell from the planes and set the house ablaze.
According to surviving kin, all three acted as if they had known they
were going to die, even though they never spoke of it.

Of the several thousand accident reports I have studied, this unusual
knowingness was present in almost all of them. Here is a summary of
what I discovered from this inquiry; it is a pattern of behavioral cues
indicating that people know, at least subconsciously, when they are
about to die:

• Anywhere from three months to three weeks in advance of the
event (perhaps even a year before), individuals begin to alter their normal behavior. There is something intense or uniquely thoughtful about
this shift.

• Subtle at first, this behavioral change becomes a desire to wrap
things up, reassess affairs and life goals, while switching from material
concerns to philosophical or spiritual ones.

• This is followed by a need to see everyone who means anything
special to them, to be friendlier, closer. If physical visits are not possible,
they make these connections by writing letters or telephoning.

• As time draws near, the people become more serious about
straightening out their affairs and instructing a loved one or a friend to

take over in their stead. This instruction can be quite specific, sometimes involving details such as debts still owed, what insurance policies exist and how to handle them, how possessions should be dispersed, and what goals, programs, or projects are yet undone and how to finish them. Financial matters seem quite important, as is the management of personal and private affairs.

• Typically, about twenty-four to thirty-six hours before death, individuals relax and are at peace. They often appear as if "high" on something because of their heightened alertness, easy confidence, and sense of joy. They exude an unusual strength and positive demeanor as if they were ready at last for something important to occur.

You may not think that this pattern applies also to infants and toddlers, but I suggest to you that it does. I have found that little ones, in ways unique to their size and physical development, are quite capable of expressing how they feel and what's on their minds; if old enough, they do it through their drawings.

This was certainly true with our granddaughter Myriam. I am struck that her mother, Lydia, knew while she was pregnant that the child would not live long. She repeatedly had dreams, as Myriam grew, that she would run away and never return; she also had visions and flashes of her lying in a hospital bed. In her last dream, mere weeks before the child died, Myriam rode up an escalator as high as she could go and then disappeared into a brilliant light—with nary a backward glance. None of us knew about this, as Lydia kept these dreams secret until after Myriam died. It was no secret, however, that Myriam herself changed three months before her seizures: she was strangely listless and ate little; photos taken of her were utterly black; there were several near misses in accidents that could have killed her; and she made people uncomfortable because of how she stared "through" and past them as if searching their souls. Her previously happy disposition had just begun to return when all but two family members unexpectedly began to grieve. I was one of them. None of us knew why we were grieving or for whom. She died shortly after our grief spells suddenly ceased.

I have observed that intuitive knowing about imminent death not only readies people to meet life's end, but more importantly it assists

∞

them in preparing loved ones and friends. Exceptions are those who display no such behavioral cues in advance of their demise. Still, I never cease to be amazed at how commonplace this pattern is and how perfectly natural is our link to the spirit world.

By the way, Myriam came back after she died. Many of us saw or sensed her. Each night for two weeks following her death she snuggled up in her older brother's bed, chatted awhile, then slept with him so that he wouldn't be traumatized by her quick departure. He talked about her visitations at breakfast each morning; when he no longer needed her, she quit coming.

Well known in the medical field is the fact that the vast majority of grieving parents have a post–death reappearance of their child. Invariably, that visit is to reassure them that their child is fine. Not just little ones, like Myriam, come back. So, too, do adults.

Linda Puig of Kentucky shared this with me about her husband, Frank:

> Seven years ago he had a bright light appear under a door he could not open. This experience followed open heart surgery. He always said he would get in the next time because it was so peaceful. For seven years we joked about this. "Be sure you knock the next time you see the door," I would tell him. On February 6, he did. I've had many lovely dreams about this wonderful man that have made perfect sense, since his departure. Most recently was in October, a few days before his cat died. I told my mother that he was coming for his cat (the cat had been sickly). Mom laughed. A few days later she cried when it happened.
>
> This darling man has "guided" his family through some difficult circumstances since his death. One of my daughters had an eight-pound ovarian cyst removed plus an ovary, and we felt his presence with her. This past July our son had a most devastating motor vehicle accident and survived. Despite a moderate brain injury, he has made a miraculous recovery. Frank was with him, too. I find it truly amazing how the departed still love and care for their family from the other side.

Again and again I have seen that, even if foreknowledge is ignored, our actions and the happenstance of snap decisions can still be guided as if *another force* were intervening in our behalf. We know when we're going to die because, in being born, we set in motion a plan arranged at a higher level of consciousness—the realm of the soul.

The soul exists. It is real, and I have seen it.

4

Inner Self Helper

"The soul refuses all limits."—*Ralph Waldo Emerson*

I'd like to tell you about what happened during two hypnotic sessions I conducted in my days as a hypnotherapist in private practice specializing in past-life regressions.

The daughter of a woman I knew proved to be an excellent subject. She had no agenda, just the desire to see if she could do it—be hypnotized. Much to my surprise she went deep fast and changed characteristics instantly. No longer was she the young woman I knew, but an Englishman in every respect, older in years, and obsessed with moving from his flat overlooking the Thames River in London to a dreary cottage in Ireland. Through hypnosis he was revealed as a successful barrister who became a judge, then promptly retired, much to the shock of those who knew him. Unmarried, he had engaged his housekeeper in sorting through a library of books and papers, fine paintings, and other possessions of taste and style. He determined who would get what, saving but

∞

a small pile for himself.

As my session with him advanced, he spoke of taking what was left to Ireland. In the center of the tiny house he had purchased there, he placed a large, comfortable rocking chair and spent the rest of his days in that chair reading his favorite books, until he died from the cancer that had been growing inside him. What made this hypnotic session so different, even traumatic, was what occurred after the man expired.

Regressionists on occasion will allow their client to experience the death they underwent in a given life, perhaps even the funeral, if it seems appropriate in helping that person gain a better understanding of any issue that might be troubling him or her. I had no choice in this case. Suddenly, the man manifested himself as a distinct energy form apart from the now-silent young woman, yet hovering over her. Still another energy form took shape to my left. I could plainly see and hear both forms. Soon they started yelling at each other, screaming, I should say. I was dumbfounded. Nothing in my training or years of practicing hypnotherapy had prepared me for this.

The second form claimed to be the man's mother. She had been waiting for this moment to face her son so that she could explain to him why she had given him away soon after his birth. His hatred for her was so vile, his opposition to her sobbing pleas so unreasonably strident, that I forced the issue and became a mediator, giving each ample time to speak while the other had to listen.

The story that tumbled out was a sad one. She, a poor barmaid in Ireland, had been raped by a customer, then shunned, as if the rape had been her fault. She had no family and barely subsisted, giving birth in a dirty hovel. Her boy child was a wonder, deserving she felt of a better life and a good future, so she placed him in a basket and left it on the front steps of an orphanage in a nearby town. She died of starvation soon after, wracked with the guilt of having to abandon her baby.

His life in the orphanage had been cruel. He was belittled often for being a castaway and teased about his mother, with taunts that even she couldn't stand him. He ran away as soon as he was strong enough, stole aboard a boat, and landed in England. Resourcefulness won him a series of jobs and enough schooling to apprentice in a law firm. A talent with debates and clever political posturing guaranteed him a lucrative career, but no time for women, which suited him just fine as he didn't especially like females. When illness cut short his ambition, he picked as the place to die the cottage that was directly in front of the orphanage where he had once lived. He notified them of his action and promised funds. It was the orphanage staff who found his body and buried him.

Once both entities had a chance to speak, a profound healing and reconciliation took place. The energy forms evaporated when my client regained consciousness. Her eyes seemed as big as saucers as she launched a volley of "oh-my-goshs." She had hated her mother since childhood, without any logical reason to feel that way; she had been drawn to law in college and excelled on the debating team; and she never had a love relationship that interested her, preferring study to dates. The next morning she and her mother listened to an audiotape of the actual regression. The last part between mother and son did not record; only my words could be heard. But to them that was enough. Again, a profound healing and reconciliation occurred; the past had become the present so that an old wrong could be righted. The intensity of reactions, the utter realness of the session, challenged everything I thought I knew about life and death, reincarnation, and time and space.

Not long after, a young man from northern California made an appointment with me. He, too, was curious about hypnosis and whether or not there was anything to the notion of past lives. He was unusually receptive and quickly slipped into a deep trance. His consciousness shifted to life in ancient Greece where he captained a large army. A patriot, he relished all aspects of war and soldiering, from torturing spies to killing hordes. He also took great pride in his wife and four children, remaining as faithful to them as he was to his calling. He died in what for him was the glory of battle after thirty years of defending his sovereign.

Next, my client moved in consciousness to a life at the foot of the high Himalayas, where, as an itinerant healer, he roamed from village to village with little but a beggar's bowl and the rags on his "toothpick" of a body. He never had a love affair or fathered children, but delighted instead in the opportunity to help others, which he did for thirty years. While stumbling along a mountain road one day, he suddenly collapsed. No one offered a hand. He died as if he were but a wad of dust hardly distinguishable from the dirt under foot and sandal.

I was aghast at the story the hypnotized man relayed. So, before I brought him back to full consciousness, I decided to try an experiment. I wanted to see if I could make contact with the all-knowing voice that spoke to me through his mouth. That voice wasn't like the ones I had heard from previous clients. It was wiser, special. I verbally requested permission to do this, unsure of "who" or "what" might answer.

Immediately, the room in which the session took place, with me sitting in a chair and him outstretched on a sofa, became incredibly hot. Although it was night, everything began glowing with a light far brighter than that provided by any of the lamps. A voice spoke that seemed to emanate from a source other than the man's lips and it permeated every cell in my body. I searched the air around me for the source of the voice, but nothing caught my eye.

"What do you want?" it boomed. I hesitated; then, gathering my strength, I asked, "The two lives just described to me, what do they mean?" A roar of laughter that seemed to shake the very walls preceded these cryptic words: "Thirty years killing. Thirty years healing. Now, all is well." Nothing more was offered. The session ended. The man "woke up." Yet he never looked or acted quite the same after that, nor did I. I was deeply affected by this session and the one before it, so much so that I eventually closed my practice of hypnotherapy.

I decided to initiate my own "inner journey to the truth of being." I knew from my earlier studies and through the activities of "Inner Forum" (a nonprofit organization I had incorporated in the state of Idaho to educate the public on the difference between exaggerated and evidential claims of the paranormal), that what unites the human family and all of creation lies within the heart of each person—internal to us, not external.

Our core self, what I discovered to be resident deep inside every client who ever came to me, was later termed by other professionals as our "Inner Self Helper" or "ISH." "Multiple personalities," wherein a single individual behaved as if more than one personality-self possessed him or her, was the research venue from which this term emerged. Almost invariably, the cause of this mental disorder was traced to child abuse. What puzzled researchers, though, was the consistent presence of a knowing and wise, stable, self-organizing "self" always found as central to each person's being. This Inner Self Helper, the one all else revolved around, I came to recognize as the soul.

My journey inward to verify this and other spiritual truths took me to places I was not prepared to go—through death's curtain. I died three times within a span of three months, and each time I experienced a near-death scenario. Each was different, yet one experience somehow led into the next as in a progression.

A miscarriage and severe hemorrhaging caused death number one, on January 2, 1977. I died again on January 4 when a large blood clot in a vein in my right thigh dislodged. Because of what I experienced, I became "lost between worlds," unable to reclaim my place in the life I once had. This inability to relate was a major factor in leading to the collapse I suffered on March 29, when my body ceased functioning and I died a third time. Never was I hospitalized, although it is obvious in looking back that I should have been.

Bits and pieces of what happened to me are in all my books: a more in-depth account about my three deaths is included in *Coming Back to Life*, and many of the revelations that were given to me are recalled in *Future Memory*. No one book contains the whole of it. My passion has been research, not storytelling. In all fairness, though, I'll fess up—at least a little.

5

When I Died

"When I hear somebody sigh, 'Life is hard,' I am always tempted to ask, 'Compared to what?'"—*Sydney J. Harris*

I didn't recognize death when I died the first time.

One minute I was standing in front of the toilet staring at a somewhat whitish-looking sac I had just passed. Blood was splattering everywhere while a pain like a hot poker pierced my heart, clamped my gut, and loosed a scream I could not identify as mine. The next minute I was bobbing along the underside of the ceiling, drawn to the light fixture with a bright, switched-on bulb inside. Like a moth to a flame, I would bump that bulb again and again before I paused long enough to look around. The bloody body on the floor meant nothing to me, except for the difference in space relations. Suddenly, it was a long way down to the toilet, sink, and bathtub. How did that happen? How could the ceiling be scarcely an eyelash away?

Never was there darkness. All my faculties were alert, heightened. Pain vanished. As I began to question what might be going on, "blobs" formed in the air around me. I didn't know what else to call these strange shapes. They were dark gray, misshapen things that looked like ink blots, but fully dimensional and buoyant. In nothing flat, the air was full of them. I heard an audible "snap," then felt myself jerked back into my body like an overstretched rubber band when it's suddenly released, entering through the top of my head where my "soft spot" had been as a baby and feeling myself shrink in size so that I would once again fit the confines of my physical form. A strong pulling sensation ensured that I made it all the way back in. Back to the pain. Back to the mess.

That's how my three deaths started—with a miscarriage and a doctor who paid no attention to the symptoms I presented when I collapsed in his office after being barely able to drive the five blocks from my home to his door. Without reading my chart and shaking with laughter that I could be taken advantage of so easily by a man I hardly knew (I was raped), he gave me an injection in my right thigh to stop the hemorrhage and sent me home. The instant I hobbled across my threshold the bleeding stopped but both legs began to hurt, especially the right. In too much pain to think straight, I headed for the bed, propped up my legs with pillows, and went to sleep. Natalie shook me awake the next morning, saying she had called my boss and reported me ill. Both girls left for school; Kelly was long gone—attending a cruise school aboard a square-rigger in the Atlantic Ocean.

I did recognize death the second time.

The specialist who later examined me fixed the cause as a large blood clot that had dislodged in a vein in my right thigh along with the worst case of phlebitis he had ever heard of, let alone seen. He kept saying, "There's no way you can be alive." I could not respond. He scribbled out a prescription and sent me home to recover, stating that in his opinion the worst was over and that I should take the drug every four hours around the clock for seven days but remain in bed, legs propped up. The pharmacist warned that I had better eat before each dose or I'd get really sick. No refills were possible; the medicine was labeled "dangerous."

As I followed the doctor's instructions, I couldn't disconnect from what had occurred: my long crawl across the length of the ranch–style rental we lived in to reach the only phone we had, a wall phone in the kitchen, so that I could call for help; and the pain in my right leg that was excruciatingly cruel and unrelenting, accompanied by a red-hot lump growing out from the side of my right thigh. With my own fists I smashed that lump so it would go away and leave me alone. But I couldn't have done a worse thing. The lump, as it turned out, was a large blood clot and it burst. I sealed my fate by such foolishness. I died.

Death is a curious thing when you know at the time that you are dying. You gain an astonishing perspective if you are willing to "step aside" as a personality and assume the role of observer. This I did. Here's what followed.

I simultaneously saw and experienced my body as it lay supine, face up, on the dining–room floor, barely three feet from the phone cord–so near. As I lay there, I witnessed myself in spirit form begin to lift. The "pain waves" fascinated me. I mean, as I lifted and floated free from my physical body, I passed through a span of distance, maybe six inches or more, where the pain I felt inside my body was physically manifesting as vibrational waves outside my body. These waves looked for all the world like the mirage you see on a hot summer's day when you're walking on pavement. You think you're seeing a shimmer of water, but what you're really seeing is an illusion created by reflected heat. The pain was severe while I was passing through the waves, but once I floated free of them, presto, no pain. Another illusion.

I floated up to the light fixture, but this time the bulb was not on. I remember laughing about the light fixture, that at least it was different from the one two days before. While I took stock of my situation, I noted how superbright everything was and how much better my faculties worked. I had full mobility, yet I wasn't really free. My physical body had to be totally, utterly dead before I could leave. Don't ask me how I knew that; I just did. So I floated back down to the body on the floor and hovered, studying the body shell I had once inhabited for any hint, any twitch, heave, or nuance that life remained. Nothing. Just to be certain, I lingered a while. Still nothing. When I was satisfied that my body was dead, I yelped for joy.

You cannot compare the concerns that are present on this side of death's curtain with what is encountered on "the other side." At crossover, priorities and awarenesses switch.

In my own case, my newfound freedom was so glorious, so wonderful, I felt as if I had just been released from a prison term and was at last free to be my complete, authentic self. No more ego personality. No more paying bills or putting up with downtown traffic or counting calories or scrubbing toilets or pleasing my boss or trying to rebuild my life after the failure of a twenty–year marriage. I loved my children, but even they no longer mattered. In the joyous freedom of NOW, where I found myself, all that existed was the truth of my God–created self. I was a soul, and I was on my way "home," and I was filled with ecstasy. Then, from a place that seemed to be above my dining–room ceiling, there appeared a brilliance beyond brilliant, another world in another dimension into which I merged.

I saw and experienced many things while in this place, among them revelations about the power of thought. For example, the gray blobs I had witnessed before I now realized were *raw thought substances*, unshapen because they lacked the focus I could have provided. I discovered that thoughts really are *things*, that thinking a thought produces the energy and the substance needed for it to exist by itself. Even though most thoughts are short–lived, those we put effort into, focus on, or think intensely about become the "climate" or atmosphere we live in. What surprised me was how exact this is: that every thought we think, every emotion we feel, and every deed we do affects those around us whether we are aware of it or not; additionally, the earth, air, water, plants, and animals. We can ignore how powerful thoughts can be or pretend it isn't so and blindly stumble through our lives feeling as if we're either victim or victor or simply a "good enough person." Or we can awaken to the power we have and the responsibility that comes with that power. (I've learned since discovering this to say or think "Cancel/Reject" to "erase" thoughts, words, and feelings I don't mean or have expressed by mistake. I have also learned to face straightaway any "errors" I committed.) Taking charge of your life means just that, on all levels of being—physical, mental, emotional, spiritual.

I was reunited with my loved ones who had died before me, including a grandfather who had passed away soon after his own children were born, and I saw Jesus. Words are insufficient for me to describe the happiness I felt being back with my Elder Brother, hugging Him, dancing with Him, laughing with Him. How could I have ever forgotten His message of love and forgiveness? Asking myself that question triggered my life review. For me, it was a total reliving of every aspect of ever having been alive, and it was overwhelming. I was ashamed of some things, pleased with others. Remembering the teachings of Jesus, I affirmed and knew that I was forgiven for past mistakes and chose to return to my physical body and reactivate it. I was inspired to do a better job with the life I once had. Ever so gently, I floated back on a "carpet" of twinkling light.

When I said I couldn't disconnect from this incident, I mean just that. After receiving the medical care I needed, there I was, back in physical form again, wearing a body that was lying on the sofa, taking drugs, and eating and taking more drugs and stuffing in more food, my daughters coming and going, and all I could do was replay in my mind what had happened as if it were still happening. I wasn't fully back from the experience, and I didn't care.

Life blurred after that. My right leg refused to support weight once I could stand. Pain was constant. My brain no longer worked as it used to, yet somehow I managed to remain employed. Doctors were useless. Drugs only made matters worse. The man who impregnated me came back into my life and asked for my forgiveness. I did forgive him, and then I requested a few moments of his time as I desperately needed someone to listen to my story of what I had encountered on "the other side" of death. I needed to talk. He refused to listen, slamming the door as he left.

I died again. I know that the emotional blow of being refused was at the core of death number three. But how do you measure that? My body shut down; nothing responded. Since I knew that "the other side" was better than this one, I resolved to go there—to stay. Living in the earth plane, as far as I was concerned at that moment, wasn't worth the bother.

∞

This time, after my body fell away and all functions ceased, I floated as a spirit straight up through the ceiling, observing each molecule of matter—ceiling/floor/roof—as I passed by. This was enormously fun! I had no previous concept that ceiling tile, insulation, wood beams, and metal supports were so remarkable in the arrangement of their particles, forms, and construction. It's as if I suddenly had 360-degree, X-ray vision, and I could see everything all at once, inside and outside. After I slipped past the roof, I sped away into the night sky, unburdened, feeling forever free.

Far in the distance a slit opened up in the sky. The slit looked like a "lip of light." I was drawn to it and sucked in by a force field that seemed to emanate from within its contours. At last, I was where I wanted to be: *inside* bliss. What I beheld, though, when I surveyed this light-filled world left me stunned.

Before me loomed two gigantic, impossibly huge masses spinning at great speed and looking exactly like tornadoes. One was inverted over the other, creating an hourglass shape, but where the spouts should have touched there were instead piercing rays of pure, raw power shooting out in all directions. The top cyclone spun clockwise, the bottom counterclockwise, yet there was the presence of *three* directions in the spin of each. Their sides were somewhat bulgy considering the tremendous rate of speed evidenced by the spinning.

I floated at a height about midway in relation to the cyclones, while still faraway from them, suspended in total disbelief. The spectacle was enormous. As I stared at it, I came to recognize my former personality-self in the mid-upper-left section of the top cyclone. Even though my persona was hardly a speck in size, I could see quite clearly who I had once been, and superimposed over this version of me were all my past lives, all my future lives, and what had been my present life—all of it happening at the same time in the same space—simultaneously. Around me was everyone whom I had ever known and around them, everyone else; and the same thing was happening to each and all. I witnessed that the past/present/future were not separate sequences, but rather a multiple hologram interpenetrated by its own reflection (what happened in the top cyclone was duplicated in the bottom one—as above, so below).

The only physical movement anyone or anything made was contraction, or expansion. There was no up or down, right or left, forward or backward. There was only in and out, like breathing, as if the universe and all of creation were breathing—inhale/exhale, contraction/expansion, in/out, off/on, back and forth, motion and rest. Honestly I felt as if I were observing the wave pattern of a giant echo, and I began to question life and its meaning. Was existence really just a series of echoes upon itself, spiraling forever outward from some primeval explosion? A big bang?

As awesome as the sight was, I soon lost interest. I was tired of life and its living, and I was tired of searching for my role in the grander scheme of things. The middle, where the spouts should have touched but didn't, where that powerful, piercing energy was, where those shooting rays originated—that's where I wanted to be.

Instinctively, I knew that the middle was the centerpoint of creation, God's portal. As I moved toward it, I was engulfed by a force that I knew, *I absolutely knew*, was the presence of God. I have no words to describe what happened to me in that presence, except to say that the memory of it still causes me to weep. Instantaneously, I felt as if I knew all things. Yet even more was revealed about the inner workings of creation and consciousness, until it seemed as if I would surely burst from the sheer immensity of the knowledge pouring into me.

At that moment, I heard my son, Kelly. He had returned unexpectedly from Greece three days before and was at the Black Angus Bar that night, tossing a few drinks with his friends as he regaled them with stories of sailing aboard the *Captain Scott*. A year later he explained what happened next. According to Kelly, he had a mug of brew halfway to his lips when he jerked the glass away, jumped from his stool, and yelled, "My mother's in trouble! I have to go home and help my mother!" He ran from the bar and drove away. It was he who discovered my lifeless body in the living room.

To understand what he did next, you should know that John and I raised our children to question authority, search for their own truth, and always check internal guidance before seeking external aid. So, instead of scrambling for a phone, Kelly calmly centered himself within

∞

that wellspring of wisdom deep inside himself (we can all access that core truth) and sought for higher guidance as to what he should do. He said he heard a voice and that voice told him: "Sit opposite the body and start talking. It doesn't matter what you say, just keep talking." He did that. And I "heard" him. His voice caused me to turn from where I was—not his words, but the love in his voice, unconditional love. I knew that that kind of love existed on "the other side," but I didn't know it could be expressed and experienced here, in the earth plane.

You realize that there are times when our children know more than we do. I came back to my body because I wanted to love as Kelly did, unconditionally. I was also infused with a sense of mission. I now knew I had a job to do and I knew what that job was. Much later, I consulted several physicians about the advisability of Kelly's action. They were unanimous in suspecting that had Kelly used the phone and then waited for medics, I would have been too far gone to be resuscitated. Since sound is the last faculty to leave at death, Kelly's voice was the quickest way to reach me and the most certain.

The way back to health was difficult. I had to relearn how to stand, walk, climb stairs, run, see properly, hear properly, tell the difference between left and right, and rebuild all my belief systems. Seven months later I suffered three relapses, one of them was adrenal failure. My blood pressure reading at the time was 60 over 60. I should have been on a slab.

No one could understand why I was getting worse instead of better until friends of mine, along with a doctor devoted to natural healing, all had the same inspiration: take her to some place new that will uplift her spirit. It was early November 1977 and the place selected was the Opera House in Seattle Center. I was medicated, laid in a van, and trucked up to Seattle, Washington, to attend "The Mind Miraculous Symposium." The first speaker "paid" for the trip. He was William Tiller, a physicist at Stanford University, and his topic was "The Eternal Now."

I don't remember much of what he said, except for the end of his talk. He announced that "the eternal now," where the past/present/future existed simultaneously, was a physical reality that could be charted via physics. He then projected on a huge screen that filled the entire

∞

stage a diagram of what he thought "the eternal now" looked like. It was two massive tornadoes inverted over each other in an hourglass shape, and where the two spouts should have touched but didn't, rays of power shot out in all directions. I jumped from my seat and rushed out of the auditorium, collapsing under a foyer light. I sobbed and sobbed. I wasn't crazy after all. What I had seen was really, really real. From that moment on, my recovery was assured.

Today, I am no longer the same person I once was. How could I be?

6

The Will of the Soul

"The eye by which I see God is the same eye as the eye by which God sees me. My eye and God's eye are one and the same—one in seeing, one in knowing, and one in loving."
—Meister Eckhart

Part of why it was so difficult for me to resume living in a physical body on the earth plane is because I had so completely identified myself as a soul that anything less than that lofty "perch" in the heaven-worlds of spirit not only seemed foreign, but a mere caricature, an insult, to the divinity I now knew was mine.

I had seen the soul. I was a soul. I had been in the perfection of God's presence as a cocreator with the Creator. I had experienced the mind of God and creation as the stirring of thought in that Great Mind. As this thought stirred, I saw that an energy pulse was produced and in such a manner that its oscillating motion set up and maintained what we recognize as time and space. I was shown that the makeup of this thought was consciousness and all that resulted from its stirring bore "the mark" of its consciousness, that literally the fabric of the universe *was* consciousness. I knew then what the biblical injunction "We are made in the image and likeness of God" meant: we as souls are "marked" by our creation in the sense of what we consist of and are capable of doing. *Creation allows the One to become the many.*

It was revealed to me that each of us as a soul has free will and unlimited potential for growth and expansion. Seemingly separate and distinct, I saw the souls God created as showers of sparks, nuclei of holy fire, that spread out and expanded in waves, thought–waves, similar in movement to what happens to the wake caused by a speedboat zooming across a placid lake. The farther afield each wave projected (in a plasmalike "ocean" of etheric substance or spirit), the more the individual sparks separated from their wave, spinning off in positive and negative poles of energy charge, mimicking what caused the central pulse beat to oscillate. I observed that the nucleus of holy fire, once divided and freed from its wave, is able to take on any manner or type of existence or shape or form. Yet no matter what experiences it takes on, the nucleus spark carries within it the urge to attract unto itself that which will unify its charge (the rejoining of its positive and negative poles back into the full nuclei it once was) and fulfill its ultimate purpose (reunion with the original source). *The many ever seek to rejoin with the One.*

Here it was, Truth with a capital "T," spread out before me like a sumptuous banquet, the very blueprint of creation and all created things: me, you, everything—and I was witness to it, and what I saw was real. More than real.

I experienced, fully and completely, that each and every one of us, all of us, are holy sparks of fire at our core. Our core–self or soul appeared to me as a matrix or mass of pulsing intelligence, sometimes undulating as if wavelike, sometimes flashing or sparkling as if a power grid or circuit board of energetic particles of light. Physically, souls are infinitesimally small, hardly more than a "wink" in size; yet, each contains a power mass so intense, a consciousness so unlimited in function and potential, that it is beyond our ability as humans to fathom its makeup or design.

I saw that what resides within our earthly frame, what we think defines us as human beings, is but a "finger" of what we are, a projection from our soul's mass.

During my third near–death experience, I reached what we in research term "the realm of all knowing." This is not unusual, as many experiencers do the same thing. While there, however, other revelations were given to me and then a voice spoke. I call it "The Voice Like None Other," for I have nothing with which to compare it. My sense is that it was of God. The Voice said, "Test revelation. You are to do the research. One book for each death." I was shown what that meant and the basics of what was to be in each. Books two and three were named, not book one.

I came to know that the reason for my birth, growing up, living and dying in the manner that I did, was to do this work. I could at last recognize how the soul's will had operated in my own life: slowly, carefully, sometimes pushing, sometimes pulling, other times strangely silent, yet always and ever guiding me toward the completion of my life task. The same can be said for others, not just me.

Then I realized that what all of us call our "mission" or special role in life, our part in the grander Reality, is that contribution that is possible for us to make once we merge into or are cooperative with our soul. We can accomplish this soul–filled relationship through prayer and meditation, spiritual/religious disciplines, because of sudden transformations of consciousness like what I experienced or thanks to a simple yet sincere desire to develop spiritually. The will of every soul is to "outpicture" the Greater Will, as it is the soul that is responsible for carrying out God's plan for creation. We are separate from our Source only for as long as we think we are separate. In Truth, our connection to a higher order never ceased and it never will.

My research of near–death states began in November of 1978 after I had moved to Virginia. It was Elisabeth Kübler-Ross who identified terms and models of the near–death experience for me, which got me started. The rest you might call "fate" or "destiny," since the very people I needed to interview and study populated my life everywhere I went. I had only to turn around and there would be another one. Such meetings occurred so often and were so exactly "right on" that they were spooky. It was as if I were wearing some invisible sign on my back that read, "Tell me about your near–death experience." One Haitian taxi driver in Washington, D.C., for instance, took one look at me as I scrambled into his cab, started laughing, and squealed, "I can tell you about my death 'cause you've died, too." I hadn't said one word to the man, nor did I offer a response to his storytelling. I just listened and smiled.

I put my own episodes and what I had learned from them on a "back shelf" in my mind so that I could be as objective and detached as possible. My questions were open ended, my gaze intense, as I studied every detail of gesture and movement and eye response that the people made—just as my father had taught me to do years before. Bodies are as expressive as words, sometimes more so. Whenever possible, I visited in the experiencers' homes and had sessions with loved ones, friends, neighbors, caregivers, employers, and the like. Anyone who talked to me garnered my undivided attention. I was serious about this work.

The greater self that reflected back to me from the eyes of the thousands of adult and child experiencers I had sessions with was not only humbling, it became an invaluable source of discernment and knowledge. When you connect with the soul, you touch a spiritual intimacy we all hunger for, an intimacy we can share with one another.

It is true that some mystics term this greater self the "oversoul," to distinguish it from the spirit essence within us that we can relate to physically on a daily basis. To me, though, the soul is the soul: *in totality* as a mass of unfathomable range and scope, able to project in multiple forms and diverse manners according to its choosing; and *in part* a subtle, gentle source of strength deep inside our earthly form that animates our existence and guides us along the varied pathways we encounter during the course of earth life. We cannot lose our soul, but we can lose the individuality we developed in and through our ego personality. I've come to think of this unfortunate possibility as a "use it or lose it" proposition: when we refuse to embrace our spiritual nature (that which nurtures the soul), our potential for creative self–expression diminishes or distorts or disappears.

∞

Truly, each one of us is an immortal soul, an extension of the Divine, who temporarily resides within a carbon–based form of electromagnetic pulsations that produce a solid–appearing, visual overleaf of behavior patterns more commonly referred to as: a physical body. The real us is I AM; and what I AM everyone else is, for all of us are cells in the Greater Body, expressions of the One God. We are one with the One. Always and ever connected.

7

Greater Aspects of the Soul

"All things are connected like the blood which unites one family. Whatever befalls the earth befalls the sons [and daughters] of earth. Man did not weave the web of life, he is merely a strand of it. Whatever he does to the web, he does to himself."—*Chief Seattle*

There is no doubt that each member of creation links into a network that in turn interweaves systems that interconnect grander patterns. From the tiniest microbe to the complex universe, everything is joined and actively works to maintain the integrity of its wholeness.

A language doesn't exist that is big and bold enough to describe how awesome, powerful, beautiful this fact is. I interact on a daily basis now with these connections, networks, and patterns; yet the closest I can get to conveying what they are like is to paint a word picture of twinkling lights woven into webs of glistening threads that form a lattice of layered intelligence. Anything and

∞

everything you can imagine is within the strings of this webbing—in-terrelationships that hold creation together: our earthly bodies and our immune systems, animal and plant interdependence, weather patterns, subjective and objective states of perception, alternate realities, and multiple facets of our own reality.

Here are some examples of visible connections:

• *Pesky ants were destroyed by city planners in Southern California, and months later there were no butterflies. It seems the butterflies were dependent on the ants for part of their life cycle.*

• *Dust blowing in from the Sahara nourishes the rainforests of the Amazon. Without the dust, the rainforests suffer.*

• *A tourist concessionaire set up shop in a cave near a forest of saguaro trees in Arizona. The cave turned out to be a roosting place for Sanborn bats, which crosspollinate saguaros; ridding the cave of the bats disrupted the pollination pattern for hundreds of miles around. This jeopardized future saguaro growth and reduced their numbers by 75 percent.*

Following are some examples of invisible connections:

• *A field of crops not in proper nutritional balance will emit a sound, much like crying, which will attract to it the very insects, bacteria, and substances needed for its restoration or destruction.*

• *A human being not in proper balance physically, emotionally, mentally, and spiritually will subconsciously set up a vibrational "signal" which will attract to him or her the very diseases, accidents, or incidents necessary for that individual's redirection, rebirth, or death.*

Violence, death, the rise of cultures and climates, our individual trials and accomplishments and heartaches, begin to take on different characteristics once we shift the level of our focus. Nothing is hidden, only ignored. What we see and experience depends entirely on the angle with which it is viewed for definition. To put it another way, where we stand determines what we see. Only our attitudes, our beliefs, block us from recognizing the makeup of the world as it exists.

The revelations I was given in death showed me that we humans are in league with countless members of a universal lifestream. What is true for one aspect of this lifestream is true for another, as each reflects the other. We cannot choose a course of action or even engage in a given activity without the "ripples" of what we're doing affecting people and places and systems and things within or beyond our field of awareness. We hold the power to effect change—each one of us do—and to a much greater extent than we choose to realize.

While I was suspended at what I sensed was the centerpoint of creation during my third near-death experience, I saw the One Mind issuing forth from the weblike "fabric" of Its own consciousness as It cradled existence in the stirring of Its Thought. The scene appeared to me as if the universe were *inside a giant brain-processing thought*: the etheric plasma its nourishing fluid; gravity its blood vessels; the threaded web and superluminous particles the network for its consciousness to flow; the objects of dense matter (such as solar systems, planets, dark matter, and life forms *plus the lives they lead*) the manifestation of its thought-form potential; the stirring of its thought the oscillating pulse that creates time and space.

What I witnessed, the relationship of the whole to its many parts, makes sense if you consider that the One may need all of Itself to experience Itself; that in reality, life's passages, births, and deaths are but a continual celebration of new beginnings in a grand spiral of remembrance. This grand spiral supports the concept of reincarnation for this reason: the soul's urge is to reunite with its Creator, irrespective of time and space (which mean nothing to a soul), and to accomplish this it needs or chooses to "grow through" and "learn from" its experiences, fulfilling a will greater than its own. Because I found this to be true, I now recognize reincarnation as *the refinement and recovery of memory that has taken shape in the world of form*. What memory? That part of the central vision that we are capable of developing and carrying out—our potential.

The world's sacred scriptures assure us that we are gods in the making; for example: "I have said, You are gods; all of you are children of the most High" (Psalm 82:6); and "God becomes man in order that man might become God" (*Bhagavad Gita*).

Before he died, Jan van Ruysbroeck, a German mystic, had a profound illumination about the reason behind existence. "God in the depths of us receives God who comes to us; it is God contemplating

God." To me, this one quote combines and condenses all the world's sacred scriptures into one glorious truth and does so with elegant grace.

I know for certain that our charge as holy souls of the Most High is a glorious one. History's revelators, the various messiahs, prophets, and mystics we have been blessed with, have done their best to stand in "the light of revelation" so that they could be filled with the Holy Spirit and found worthy to receive whatever God would give. From them has come the spiritual gems that inform our lives today. But divine revelation is ongoing; there is no "club" exclusive to revelators. The illumination of Jan van Ruysbroeck proves this—that truth speakers of the highest order have spanned the ages and are in every culture, tribe, and society. What distinguishes them from the rest of us (who are occasionally blessed with insight or have a vision) is the impact their message had on the people who were transformed by it—for the better.

Our wise ones have emphasized, for the most part, that we as individuals are more powerful and capable than we seem, that our origins are divine, that the lives we lead are purposeful, and that when we are ready we can transcend this world and go to another. None has said that we were "playthings," mere puppets or possessions who lived for the amusement of the "gods"; rather, our various revelators and truth speakers have claimed that free will is ours by right of birth as a sign of God's love for us.

This ability to choose guarantees us a role as cocreators with the Creator, enjoined by the very act of creation to go forth and multiply and expand and grow. We do this through the "journeys" we take to discover and test and enjoy what we find. These journeys of life after life enable us to build "muscles," to make real the abilities we possess, fine-tuning the knowing that propels us.

Our greater self holds the curriculum that our lesser self seeks to apply. It's all the same self. The only difference between the two is one of vibration.

If this confuses you, think of electricity. Imagine all the many ways a multitude of people can plug in to an electrical current simultaneously. Then imagine that your soul is a certain voltage of that current. Just because the individual you have become is unlike what you once were in spirit does not lessen your ability to plug in at will with the fuller power that you are, nor does it diminish to any degree the amount of "juice" you can access from greater sources of higher voltages.

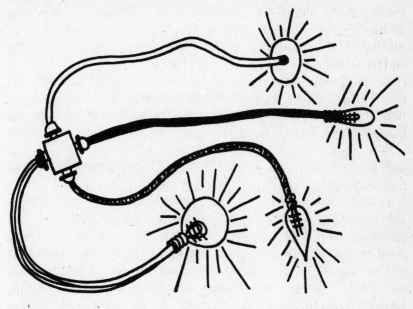

Without our existence as an individual self to experiment with possibilities, the power we have (i.e., "electrical currents") would remain unseen and little used. (Remember, electricity is only valuable if it can be harnessed, directed, and maintained in a manner that is compatible with the vibrational level that seeks its connection.)

I've learned that being a soul created by God is not enough. Without the ability to cocreate, to multiply and manifest and dream and desire, without free will, the soul would be one-dimensional, and creation would be little more than a mess of matter—if that. What makes for interest and thus diversity is the interplay of relationships and the richness of unpredictability. As souls, we were given all the gifts we needed to outpicture God's thoughts, including the ability to project or extend our spirit selves into form, to become individualized.

As an individual, we can ignore the realms of spirit and cast aside any notion of a soul or higher self, and identify only with our ego and what we witness in the physical world around us. Or we can awaken to the reality that there is something greater than the ego self, something better, and much more beyond that.

It has often been said that we create our own reality as individuals. In the sense that we have the power of invention and choice, this is true. But we can and do make mistakes, have accidents, slip up, deviate, or detour away from our goals and dreams. Since this occurs, why do our spiritual leaders insist that there are no accidents and that everything is known ahead of time? This claim runs counter to our gift of free will.

What I witnessed revealed to me that we cannot control everything that happens to us in life. Other forces intervene. But we can control our responses. We can use each incident that occurs to our advantage. Whether or not it's part of our life path, we can learn from it. We can benefit. Never is there a moment when all is lost, not even when conditions appear otherwise. We can choose again. The trick is to learn how to choose wisely. The way I deal with this is to surrender my will to God's will, to that purpose of larger import than my own. This act allows the lesser and the greater to merge. When I remember to do this, my life "flows" in a steady stream of miracles, large and small.

The right to choose does not guarantee protection or outcomes. But it does enable us to adjust to ever-changing landscapes consciously and thoughtfully. Accidents that intrude upon our life and mistakes that set us back or complicate issues are possible to overturn when we accept the responsibility we have in the decision-making process. Not to choose is still a choice.

The claim that "there are no accidents," that we alone create our reality, falls into place once we realize that because of free will we can reshape, readjust, and realign more than we think—as an individual *and* as a soul. Details can alter, outcomes can change, but the end result is always "on course," as all things sooner or later work together for the good of the whole—whether or not *we* made it happen.

Have you ever studied the chaos theory in mathematics? Briefly put, it shows how new order emerges from disorder; how no matter the extent of devastation or destruction that occurs, the various systems involved automatically mutate in ways that transform and transfigure one whole into another one as if "orchestrated." There is rhythm, grace, and beauty in whatever seems chaotic: a progressive orderliness that interweaves what appear to be "random" events.

I have recognized this phenomenon, this miracle, in the lives of people and businesses and nations and landscape expanses. Regardless of the situation, be it positive or negative, energy out of balance with itself will build up to where a "tipping point" is reached, to where circumstances get "top heavy" from the "weight" of intense pressure and stress. When this happens the situation topples over or shifts form. The law of chaos guarantees this. It is what led to the fall of the Berlin Wall, to every tyranny that ever existed, to every paradise ever built, and to every economy that ignored the growing needs of its people. Energy seeks its own balance. If something blocks this movement, something else will come along to remove the block.

In the human family, I call these "block removers" *growth events*.

Growth events come in all shapes and sizes. They can be negative or positive or both; they repeat if we miss one, or they can be a series, one right after another. Some examples of growth events are: losing when we were certain we would win, or winning when we were certain we would lose; forced to slow down when we wanted to go faster, or forced to speed up when we wanted to go slow; suffering when we wanted to prosper, or prospering when we were unprepared or even unwilling. A growth event is any kind of sudden, unexpected twist in life that twirls you around and changes your attitudes and stretches your mind.

Growth events give us an opportunity to face our inner selves and "clean house," to glimpse the collective mind and higher realities, to expand past that which limits, to discover the impossible, and experience the so-called "paranormal" (that something "extra" beyond what is typical).

The soul experiences growth events, too. I call them *learning cycles*.

This is what I learned about the learning cycles of the soul: These cycles evolve around an overall theme and are planned according to

∞

whatever is necessary to carry out and fulfill the theme. For instance, if the soul wanted to explore the nature of courage, it would plan various incidents and opportunities that would enable it as an individual of flesh and bone to embark upon such explorations. Time would not matter, since time has a different meaning to a soul than it does to a human personality.

These thematic soul cycles can be fulfilled in one lifetime, cover a series of lifetimes, or happen in different or multiple forms of existence on other levels besides that of the earth plane. Results depend on how the soul develops along the way, what it learns.

Souls can unite in groups for the initiation and carry through of a common purpose, mission, or goal. Tremendous amounts of focused energy are produced and released when souls do this, enough to influence sweeping changes in society or cause major alterations in the world at large.

Commitments like this often involve souls who choose to be born into bodies in the earth plane during the same timeframe. This enables them to either be part of each other's lives or interact with each other in significant ways that will affect the larger human condition; for example, signers of the Declaration of Independence, all men in their twenties and thirties, whose courage and intelligence made a nation out of diverse parts, and families, like the Kennedys, who, aside from being a tightly knit bunch prone to personal foibles, sponsored service-oriented projects that benefited millions. Another example is the period from the late 1800s to the early 1900s, when the synergy of inventors across the globe brought forth the industrial revolution and achieved phenomenal changes in our lives. This exact same pattern of groupings or clusters of talent played out in other fields of interest as well, making those years in history forever remembered as "earth shaking."

Groups of committed souls can "move mountains" in what they can accomplish. Those I've recognized in my research and in the spirit journeys I have taken created pivot points, major junctures, in human and planetary activity for the working-out of a greater plan. Death on a massive scale sometimes followed their efforts (i.e., the sinking of the *Titanic*; the Holocaust; September 11, 2001, when planes crashed into the

World Trade Center and the Pentagon). The reasons why have not always been mine to know, but, since my own death experiences, I have at least been able to access the inner planes of the spirit realms where the detachment necessary to appreciate the larger view is possible to attain. How I would define the "inner planes" is that dimension, that space, that resonance, wherein resides the untarnished soul (our Higher Self) and the grandness of God's wisdom.

From the inner planes, I have witnessed that when the soul or forces greater than the soul intervene in a person's life or in the spread of history, a "field effect" takes place. Science uses the term "fields" to indicate domains of influence, that which holds together in an imposed order. A practical way to demonstrate this is to scatter iron filings on a piece of paper, then hold a magnet underneath the paper. The filings will all converge in a pattern that reflects the magnet's field array. Human consciousness is no different. If collective thought fields (often termed "mass mind" or "the preference/desire of the majority") are threatened, overstressed, or deeply affected by a change in the structure that supports their stability, they will respond as the iron filings did.

Again, a magnet will pull scattered metal filings together in a manner that matches its drawing power. Similarly, an event of great impact will unite a broad span of people, events such as the bombing of Pearl Harbor, the moon landing, unusually tragic deaths, and the Civil Rights Movement. This "pulling together" activity creates field effects.

Domains of influence exist on the other side of death, too. These fields comprise what is commonly known as heaven and hell and are shaped in the ethers over time by the accumulated clustering (pulling together) of emotions, feelings, thoughts, and desires. If this seems far-fetched to you, turn the page and learn what I learned.

8

Heaven and Hell

"Out beyond ideas of wrongdoing and rightdoing, there is a field. I'll meet you there."—Rumi

Hell is just as real as heaven and, after people die, more go there than anyone wants to admit.

You can't promise folks that after death everyone goes to a paradise of green fields, lovely homes, celestial music, good food, good sex—and be honest. Such promises are far too often either misguided attempts to show love and affection or plain, old-fashioned propaganda meant to control a person's mind.

What can be promised, what I am doing here, is to share the type of testimony that is based upon personal witnessing balanced with careful research. My goal is to stretch your mind, not stuff it into another "belief box." With that said, let me offer a few "givens":

• Our greater self holds the curriculum that our lesser self seeks to apply.

∞

- What we see of what we experience in life depends entirely upon our angle of view.
- Only our attitudes and beliefs limit us.
- The journeys we take life after life enable us to build "muscles," make real the abilities we possess, and fine-tune the knowing that propels us.

These "givens" fade in significance, however, once death comes and the personality is freed from physical form to merge with the soul. Time and space disappear when this occurs.

What I found once I left the world of time and space during my own death episodes were countless realms and dimensions of existence that ranged from the slower, more dense vibrations of shape and sound (similar to being inside rocks or metal) to higher, finer streamers of nonenergetic currents and abstractions (similar to being inside a light ray or a cloud). These realms and dimensions existed in field arrays of wave forms (orderly domains). They appeared as a layered matrix. The various levels of each plane were separated from each other by frequencies of vibration. Emanations of transcendent realities pervaded throughout.

Before me, quite literally, were layers upon layers of worlds within worlds, each stacked atop the other like a "wraparound hotel of many floors." In visionary literature, the "elevators" that supposedly allow one to go up or down the various levels of the afterlife are most commonly described as stairs, columns, rays of light, great trees (roots and all), and/or pathways. I did not encounter any such imagery or mechanisms, however. In my case, I simply possessed the ability to see through things as if suddenly gifted with 360-degree, X-ray vision. I sensed the presence of twelve layers of higher, finer energies and twelve layers of slower, more dense energies. A dozen heavens. A dozen hells. Whether or not this is correct, I have no way of knowing. There were lots of them, though, a lot more than most traditions teach, and beings without number existing inside of each one.

The denser realms consisted of such levels as fiery infernos, frozen wastelands, stark nothingness, terrible storms, torture chambers, excesses of behavior, and a profound loneliness. In the finer realms, levels were closer to that which everyday people engage in in everyday living, such as mansions, breathtakingly beautiful scenery, universities, cloistered devotionals; in the higher realms, fluid beings of splashed light.

Yet none of this was really real. I could see through all of it, including the beings, as if this "layer cake of life" were nothing more than an optical illusion. The heavens and hells and the beings inhabiting them existed in the manner that they did because of the way energy operates in and through the living, breathing, pulsating fabric of consciousness.

Over time the accumulation in the ethers of people's emotions, feelings, thoughts, dreams, and desires is what creates the worlds of heaven and hell. Because of how this accumulation clusters by rate of frequency, layered bands result. These layered bands or fields stick together and form a matrix of identifiable substance, shape, and activity, as more and more "material" is absorbed into them. That is why basically the same imagery shows up across the globe in myths, dreams, visions, and journeys into spirit, with details and designs altering as societies modernize and individuals gain a broader understanding of themselves and the world around them.

I wish to repeat: These layered bands have stabilized over the eons that people have walked the earth. What each consists of is experienced as absolutely real at each level of vibration; after death, individuals in spirit form seek or are drawn to the place they "fit" or feel is right for them. The soul needs this arrangement to process, heal, cleanse, and unify what it learned during the physical sojourn just completed, so that it can continue its evolution back to Source; to become a fully conscious, individualized cocreator with the Creator.

How I define the arrangement of heaven and hell, based upon what I have observed, follows:

Hell refers to levels of negative thought forms that reside in close proximity to the earth plane. The vibration in these levels is slower, heavier, and more dense. It is where we go to work out whatever blocks us from the power of our own light: hangups, addictions, fears, guilts, angers, rage, regrets, self-pity, arrogance. We stay in hell (and there are many divisions to this vibratory level) for however long best serves our development. There is no condemnation here, per se, rather the work-

∞

ing out of our own errors in judgment and mistakes, misalignments, or misappropriations (commonly referred to as "sin"). In hell, we have the opportunity to either revel in our folly or come to grips with the reality of consequences: that every action has a reaction and what is inflicted on another can be returned in kind. We experience the flip side of our despair or our demands, living through the extremes of whatever we dread. This is not a punishment for our sins as much as it is a confrontation with distortions of our values and priorities. We do not leave the realms of hell until we have changed our attitudes and perceptions and are ready for another chance to improve and advance.

Heaven describes levels of positive thought forms that reside in close proximity to the earth plane. The vibration of these levels is faster, lighter, and more subtle. It is where we go to recognize or enjoy whatever reveals the power of our own light: talents, abilities, joys, courage, generosity, caring, empathy, givingness, virtue, cheer, diligence, patience, thoughtfulness, lovingkindness. We stay in heaven (and there are many divisions to this vibratory level) for however long best serves our development. There is a sense of benefit here, as if one has found one's true home and all is well (commonly referred to as recess or a time of reaping rewards). In heaven, we have the opportunity to assess our progress as a soul, to evaluate pros and cons and outcomes, to remember all truths, including that of our real identity. We experience the glory of love and the power of forgiveness, and we come to realize our purpose in creation's story: how we fit and what possibilities exist for future learning and growth. We do not leave the realms of heaven until we have advanced as an awakened soul, unified in the spirit and consciousness of love.

Neither heaven nor hell is an end point. Eternity is more vast than either one and far more wondrous. No one knows how vast it is, for all any of us have ever been given are glimpses.

I did observe "borderlands" or "shadowlands," distinct from the domains of heaven and hell, where individuals in spirit form can tarry. Sometimes the ego personality refuses to merge with the soul at death and remains somehow "apart." This situation can be temporary or long lasting, caused most often by the intensity of an individual's desire not to leave or perhaps from disorientation or confusion, feeling lost, or maybe because of a vow or a promise.

Those in the shadowlands have not detached from the earth plane or the life they had here. There are "way stations" at this vibration, places/beings/angels ready to help new arrivals deal with conflicting feelings or deeply held desires. Also, many religious and spiritual traditions make allowance for such "death distress" by encouraging the living to pray for the departed, so any that are lost may be found.

While deep in trance, the gifted psychic Edgar Cayce spoke of "akashic records" or "The Book of Life." Numerous mystical traditions teach of this, a book wherein an individual's thoughts, words, and deeds are recorded and kept, like everyone else's, in a type of heavenly library. I never saw an actual book or library on "the other side," but I did encounter what Cayce went on to describe:

These as we find are not as material records, but are upon the skein of time and space—or the akashic records.   1223-4

For the light moves on in time, in space, and upon that skein between same are the records written by each soul in its activity through eternity; through its awareness, through its consciousnesses; not only in matter but in thought, in whatever realm that entity builds for itself in its experience, in its journey, in its activity.   815-2

The akashic records appeared vibrational to me, as Cayce had indicated. When I reached the frequency where they existed, I instantly found myself "inside" them, reliving my life in full import, including the effect I had on others and on the environment. Among what I learned from this experience is that each of us, as the author of our own story, can change things. The power of forgiveness that we have available to us is quite real; eternal damnation is not.

Of immense interest to us at this point is the work of George W. Meek, a research scientist with a brilliant mind who devoted his retirement to searching for evidence of an afterlife. His book *After We Die, What*

Then? is both an overview of research on the subject (as of 1980) and a primer on his invention of the first electronic equipment capable of achieving *direct dialogue* with purported beings from the spirit realms. His careful and detailed analysis of the communications that came through his "Spiricom" revealed a field array of planes said to exist on "the other side" of death that dovetails with what I witnessed. During discussions the two of us had back in the '80s, he agreed that vibrational resonance must be what determines where we go after dying (like attracts like). Still, he could find nothing that indicated we remained where we went indefinitely, nor could I.

Meek was able to identify at least eleven main sections or levels to the afterlife as a result of his work. Here is a brief summary of what he discovered:

First Level, Physical Earth Plane—While still alive, we have a physical body as well as an interpenetrating, nonphysical etheric body, and an astral body. The etheric is the energy blueprint that supports the physical body and dies when the physical body does. The astral holds the soul during its sojourn and can travel to other planes.

Second Level, Lowest Astral Plane—This is the equivalent of emotional excesses, demonic possession, and the various realms of hell.

Third Level, Intermediate Astral Plane—Similar to the earth except lovelier, with many opportunities to rest, rehabilitate, and learn.

Fourth Level, Highest Astral Plane—The "summerland" of heaven, with angelic assistance and unconditional love. Wider perspectives about life are gained, and greater vistas to creation are revealed.

Fifth and Sixth Levels, Mental and Causal Planes—Unlimited development of mind and soul, with access to all accumulated wisdom. The final opportunity for rebirth into the earth plane is available, as further advancement leads to the celestial realms where that option is no longer relevant.

Seventh Level, Celestial Plane—Biblically referred to as "the seventh heaven," contact with the Godhead readily occurs here. The secrets of miracles and creation itself are given.

Eighth Level, First Cosmic Plane—The last plane in our solar system and the one where "at-one-ment" with the Godhead is possible.

Ninth Level, Second Cosmic Plane—The end of manifest, vibratory creation.

Tenth Level, Third Cosmic Plane—The void, nonvibratory or pure consciousness.

Eleventh Level, Fourth Cosmic Plane—Full "at-one-ment" and entry into states of consciousness beyond human comprehension.

Now that Meek has passed on, Mark Macy continues his work in the new field of study called Instrumental Trans-Communication or ITC. Like all new endeavors, ITC has had its growing pains. This struggle is depicted, fairly and objectively, in Macy's *Miracles in the Storm*. He points out in his book that the reason that so many researchers have been challenged to progress from obtaining barely audible spirit voices recorded on audiocassette tapes to fully involved, real-time, direct dialogue between beings in heaven and those on earth is that they relied solely on technical expertise and ignored the spiritual. It is his belief that without participants dedicating their efforts in service to the highest good of all humankind, results will continue to be either inconsistent or nonexistent.

Explorations of the edge of death like Meek's and Macy's have spawned yet another avenue of study, termed "after-death communications," by Bill Guggenheim and Judy Guggenheim. In their book, *Hello from Heaven: A New Field of Research Confirms That Life and Love Are Eternal*, the Guggenheims recounted over 2,000 interviews with those who said they were contacted in some manner by their loved ones after his or her death. Based on their findings, they estimated that at least 50 million Americans or 20 percent of the population have had one or more experiences with after-death communications. They found these contacts to be credible and not the product of fantasy or illusion.

We survive death as the deathless souls we are and have always been. We can be contacted, seen, and heard after we die. Of the thousands of stories I have been told about contacts between the living and the dead, here are a few that indicate how common such stories are and how broad ranging:

Ellen Lively Steele, New Mexico—"A dear friend went over recently. Franklin and I had studied together twenty-odd years ago and he truly was a special individual (for a man!). His memorial service was a celebration of his life, not his death. No tears, just joy. I didn't go to the cemetery—just came home to work on my grandson's afghan. It got dark and I turned on the pole lamp behind my chair so that I could see better. After a while (keep in mind I am alone except for a couple of cats), the light switch on the lamp clicked 'off.' I started to get upset and then decided I had better ask who it was. I heard laughter and giggles (he loved a practical joke). When I acknowledged that it was he, the light switch clicked two times, bringing the lamp back into bright."

Betty Anderson, Australia—"My sister rang me and said that when she went to the hospital to see Granny, she hugged her. Granny hugged? No, never; she would never do that. But she did and told my sister that a man appeared at the end of her bed and told her to get ready as he was coming back tomorrow to take her to see her mother. But her mother has been dead for forty years. The nurse said Granny's health was good; she will live another few years. But the next day he came and took her. Her death was a month before her 107th birthday.

While in a cemetery in Too-woombe, I kept hearing someone calling my name. I followed the sound and found the grave of a dear friend of our family, who had passed away without our knowledge."

Frank Monteleone, New York City area—"My young son died of cancer eight years ago. If you are a parent, I need not say anything else. Just weeks before his passing, I remember waking in the dead of night and even though I was still in bed, I was instantly in my family room. I was not a body standing, but rather I felt like two eyes only. It's difficult to explain. In any event, I am looking straight ahead at the other end of the room and my deceased father is standing there. He is dressed in his white dress shirt, just like always, and my son (his grandson) is in front of him. My dad looks sad and is talking to me without moving his lips. His hands are on my son's shoulders and he is saying, 'Garrett will not make it, but try not to worry. All things will work out. I will be here for him when his time comes.' It was very upsetting and not what I wanted to see or hear. The next thing I remember, I am awake in bed staring at the ceiling and not believing what had happened. A few weeks later, my son passed on. Prior to his passing, he had been working on a project to transfer old family Super8 movies to video. My wife and I put the tape in the VCR one night after his death and were overcome when the very first footage is a tape of my dad holding Garrett in his arms at the age of two or three. They are both waving at me, my dad in *the same white shirt,* happy as can be and saying, 'Hello, we're fine and everything is great here.' To say I was overcome would not nearly be sufficient."

On television news some time ago, a brief spot was aired about a young mother of two small daughters who lost her husband in the attack on the World Trade Center on September 11th. The piece was about coping with loss. The mother noted that sometimes when they are just sitting around talking, one of her daughters will look past her into the air and say, "Hi, Daddy," and then carry on a conversation with him.

Of all the nurses, counselors, and physical therapists I have spoken with in the last twenty-four years, who work with children injured in the same accident that killed their parents, the majority admitted that the kids physically saw and verbally spoke with their parents on a daily basis until released from intensive care. Also these kids knew all about the accident and that their parents were dead, even though no such details were ever communicated to them until much later.

Children can see through the veils of spirit, especially if there is a need. Generally they do not lose this ability until embarrassed, put down, or made fun of by classmates, teachers, or relatives during the early years of school.

Another note to remember is that when time and space disappear in death, so does sequencing. Simultaneity is the natural state of an evolved soul. Souls are not limited in their advancement by a single body that engages in a single progression of activity. They live in a *multi*-verse , not a *uni*-verse. That means that trips through heaven and hell can be accomplished in the "wink of an eye," in a single journey, in many journeys, or through multiple journeys simultaneously experienced. Whether they are slow or fast seems to depend on how loving and compassionate we become while on earth. Putting spiritual values first in life enables the soul to "overlight" the ego. We become who we really are when that happens.

9

The Breath of God Breathing

The Spirit of God has made me, and the breath of the Almighty gives me life."—*Job 33:4*

I have seen the soul thought–waves; they are beautiful beyond beauty, lustrous and shimmering, gloriously luminous and radiant, musical. And, oh, the tones of their music! To hear the sounds of their tones is to forsake all else forever, save the memory of God.

In a strange kind of way, J.R.R. Tolkien wrote of this celestial music and of the soul thought–waves, only he couched his story in mythic imagery for his book, *The Silmarillion*, a prequel to his celebrated trilogy *The Lord of the Rings*. Find a copy and read the first four pages of the chapter entitled "The Music of the Ainur." There is no need to quote his text here except to say that Tolkien used the idea of musical tone waves as a representation of the stirring of God's thought, to explain how creation poured forth, and how from the themes of God's thought harmonics the created

∞

"holy ones" (souls) produced and manifested their own diversions; melody being an expression of "good," dissonance, "evil."

As Tolkien's book describes the beginnings of creation and the separation of the holy souls from the mind of God, the children's movie *The Dark Crystal* illustrates the reconnection possible once the holy souls reunite with their original charge (the nucleus as it existed before dividing into positive and negative poles of energy), and return to Source. (Treat yourself. Rent a video and watch the movie.)

Certainly, this marvel of puppet wizardry runs through typical themes of good and evil, sacrifice and greed, but it emphasizes as well that neither duality is valid, that appearances can deceive. In the closing frames of the movie, the evil monsters and the blessed wise ones merge into each other (the nucleus spark rejoins with its opposite charge), and a tremendous burst of light and power is released (the reconnection). From this brilliance, the radiant whole and reunified souls go back to the God from whence they came, and the planet is restored to harmony.

Tears flooded my eyes when I saw this movie, for it so perfectly expresses how limited and narrow viewpoints can obscure the greater truths witnessed by those who slip beyond "the veil" that supposedly separates the spirit worlds from the earth plane. Granted, because of societal conditioning, it is difficult to defy family or group consensus (the will of the majority). During our brief span on earth, we tend to develop our egos to such a degree that no other destiny save death's darkness seems possible for us. However, awakenings, even if only brief or partial, change this.

The bias of belief gets peeled away in the "light of enlightenment" that can come from a near-death experience or a spiritual transformation or a religious conversion or any type of enlightening episode that deeply impacts the individual involved. Afterward, astonished individuals may exclaim such expressions as: "I now understand why my daughter died"; or "So that's why he lost an arm"; or "I was shown the real reason behind the war." As a result of these revelations—that life's many puzzle pieces do indeed fit together, that there is a greater plan, and that each individual has a place in that plan—most return to everyday living

∞

with a sense of peace that they never before thought possible.

It has been my observation that transformative events (irrespective of type) alter our perception. Because of this, our view of reality expands to accommodate concepts and ideas that once seemed foreign or foreboding or just so much nonsense. Some experiencers of transformative states (like near–death episodes) are more deeply affected than others, of course, but all are touched to a degree.

What is amazing, though, is that almost to a person experiencers return knowing that "God is, death isn't," a realization of profound significance.

I'd like to share with you what it was like for me and countless others to be bathed in "the light like none other" that we encountered during our near–death experiences.

That light is the very essence, the heart and soul, the all–consuming consummation of ecstatic ecstasy. It is a million suns of compressed love dissolving everything unto itself, annihilating thought and cell, vaporizing humanness and history, into the one great brilliance of all that is and all that ever was and all that ever will be.

You know it's God.

No one has to tell you. You know.

You can no longer believe in God, for belief implies doubt. There is no more doubt. None. You now *know* God, and you know that you know—and you're never the same again.

You know who you are: a child of God, a cell in the greater body, an extension of the One Force, an expression from the One Mind. No more can you forget your identity or deny or ignore or pretend it away.

There is One, and you are of the One.

One.

The light does this to you.

It cradles your soul in the heart of its pulse beat and fills you with loveshine. You melt away as the "you" you think you are, reforming as the "you" you really are, and you are reborn because at last you "remember."

Not all speak of God when they return from their experience as I have related here, but the majority do. That majority reports that being in the presence of God or of God's great light was the "ultimate or-gasm"—a state of intense, ecstatic, exhilarating upliftment that was so overpowering to them that they felt that if they remained there too long, they would surely be blown asunder by the sheer force of the energy it emanated.

Child near-death experiencers, even tiny tots, had a way of shaking or rocking their bodies when trying to convey this experience during our sessions. On occasion some of them would suddenly glow, shudder all over with eyes rolled up and back, mouth parted, as if in the throes of a similar energy surge. I paid special attention to this peculiar reaction because, whenever I was able to make follow-up visits once the children were older, those who had displayed that response went on to describe having had a direct contact of some kind with God. (Vestiges of this reactive behavior also showed up in some of the children's draw-ings.)

Although near-death states can be incredibly meaningful and en-lightening to anyone of any age, I did not find any other element in the story line of episodes that had quite this impact: no angel appearance, bright light, judgment tribunal, or heavenly St. Peter; only the presence or light of God. I use the word *presence* to signify a curiosity: Of the people in my research base who saw God as a manifested being (usu-ally male), most felt, regardless of age, that what they had seen was really a disguise, an overleaf, or a temporary "covering" to what was actually there—a force of unspeakable power. Some were brave enough to ask the manifested form, "Is that what you really look like?" Without exception, the being would then burst into a sphere or ball of light so immense that it was beyond the scope of language to describe.

I am still comfortable using the term *God* when referring to deity, but many are not. Popular substitutions are "That Which Is Nameless" or "The Force" or "The One Mind," or, as referenced in the Bible as the true name of God—"I Am That I Am." Clearly, after such an episode, the individual's concept of God radically alters.

This sudden burst into a ball or sphere of light occurred as well when angelic beings were asked about the realness of their form. In those cases where both angels and God changed their appearance during a single near-death scenario, everyone I spoke with who witnessed such a thing maintained that the angelic light, as awesome as it was, did not compare with God's light. One individual, who attempted to make a comparison between the two, said that the ball of light an angel became was as grand as the brightest star; yet when God changed form, the light burst that followed equated to the power of at least ten thousand suns (others insisted that the range was more on the order of a million suns).

There is no question in my mind that the near-death experience itself consists of or is based upon a force so strong that people can be changed physically as well as psychologically. Physical changes reported the most often include a sudden sensitivity to light and sound afterward, a reversal of body clocks, expanded faculties, substantially lower blood pressure, a decreased tolerance of standard pharmaceutical and chemical agents, heightened intelligence and/or creative and intuitive abilities, alterations to some degree in the nervous and digestive systems, electrical sensitivity, and multiple sensing (for example, "hearing color" or "seeing sound"). Psychological changes involve such characteristics as loss of the fear of death, becoming more loving and compassionate, less concerned with materialistic goals, more spiritually inclined, occupational switches to those jobs that are more service or healing oriented, comfortable with what seemed intolerable before, loss of time constraints, a charisma that seems to "charm" others (sometimes even creatures in the wild), less stressed, and a sense of "knowing" that can increase over time.

The degree to which these changes occur depends upon the intensity of the episode: the greater the intensity, the greater the spread of aftereffects. As these changes may not be easily handled or adjusted to, my finding that it takes a minimum of seven years for near-death experiencers to integrate the aftereffects has now been clinically verified by Dutch cardiologist Pim van Lommel and his associates in a prospective study published in *The Lancet*.

No revelation of itself can do this. A unique patterning of energy is involved in near-death states, an all-consuming depth of feeling and sensation that sets this phenomenon apart from drugs, dreams, halluci-

∞

nations, oxygen deprivation, channelings, visions, fantasy, temporal lobe seizures, and wish fulfillment.

Many adult experiencers of near–death states claim that during their episode it seemed as though the whole universe and all of creation were breathing, that in reality the only movement anything or anyone made was expansion and contraction (inhalation/exhalation). To them, breathing came to represent the stirring of God's thought as it reverberated throughout an ever–expanding field of conscious awareness, commonly termed "creation," and sustaining as it did the stage where our dramas, our roles, our endeavors, and our dreams of who we are are arranged and played out. Comments that child near–death experiencers gave during sessions I had with them included this offering: "Spirit is everywhere, like air, and it breathes, but not like our nose does. That means everything breathes. I do. You do. So does God. God's breath is what keeps the universe alive."

There is precedence for what modern–day near–death experiencers, as well as myself, report. That precedence can be found, oddly enough, in the historical concept behind the evolution of certain word meanings from various cultures, particularly as it relates to the word *spirit*.

Originally *spirit* meant "essence" or "breath." Yet, all three words have been used interchangeably as if they each referred to the same thing. This makes a tremendous difference conceptwise with interpretations of meaning. For instance, when we say we're being spiritual, the inference is that we have chosen to live in "the fullness of breath's essence." When we speak of spirituality, we are actually describing "the source from whence the pureness of breath comes." Spirit realms, if we continue further with this line of thinking, exist as "source places of pure essence," while spirit beings become "visitors or emissaries from source places of pure essence."

See what happens? If you regard "spirit" in light of its original meaning, everything alters: our view of ourselves, our beliefs and emotions, the breath we breathe, and reality itself.

I find it intriguing when Holy Spirit is reinterpreted in this manner. Numerous biblical scholars have done it and come up with: "The Breath of God Breathing." When I discovered this definition, it triggered all

∞

kinds of memories and associations for me. Mainly because, as I have already indicated, during my near–death experiences I had the distinct sensation that the universe and everything therein was alive and breathing, that breath was what moved the creative fire, and that in between the motion of God's breath lay the centerpoint of Truth—ever hidden, yet ever exposed.

But there's more. Native peoples the world over emphasize verbs over nouns in their speech, placing the emphasis on *relationship* rather than on object. If you keep this in mind, the various Native American names for deity or God actually translate to something like "Thinks Breath Creates" or "Dwells Above Great Breathing." Our notion that tribal terms for *God* always mean "The Great Spirit" bypasses entirely the truth these people seek to convey. To a native speaker, *God* is a verb that denotes the relationship between the essence of breath (sourcing) and the act of breathing (connecting with sourcing). Accordingly, then, all kingdoms and all worlds spiral around the same "great breathing" (what I encountered at the centerpoint).

The link then between spirit and breath and essence weaves together into one fabric the tapestry we call "existence," a tapestry we can better appreciate if we reduce its scope to the basic function of breathing in, breathing out.

Do that now. Take a deep breath.

Notice that a deep breath calms your nerves and perks up your brain. It's not just the added oxygen we take into our lungs that does that, but the circulation of that oxygen. Breath movement is the most common criterion we have for determining aliveness, perhaps on "the other side" as well.

After my near–death experiences I was challenged to relearn the simple art of breathing. In so doing I rediscovered the aliveness possible for a soul inhabiting a physical body on the earth plane. I had already witnessed the fuller significance of breath while I was on "the other side" and, in a way, that coincided with the language development of the world spirit. My task at the time was to transfer this greater knowing to the physical and, in a practical manner, that would make a positive difference in my ability to reclaim my place as an individual

∞

who was alive and well. The result was this revelation: How a person holds his or her fingers determines to a large extent how the air flows into each lobe of the lungs.

Anyone who practices yoga learns this, that there are certain finger positions that can be used to direct and control the air we breathe. The research that backs this up is impressive. The technique is best learned in a yoga class; still, one of these finger positions is more valuable in more ways than most teachers mention—the position for low-chest breathing.

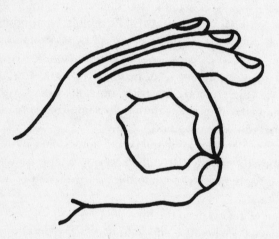

As depicted in this drawing, the tips of your index finger and thumb touch lightly to create a circle, while the other fingers hang loose and open.

Placing the fingers of both hands in this position automatically enables the air we breathe to fill all five lobes of our lungs. At the same time, it grounds or stabilizes the air in the lower lobes, located just above the diaphragm and solar plexis (the midpoint in our bodies). Putting your fingers this way as often as you can (while watching a movie or television show, while taking a walk, while meditating, etc.), for at least six months and once in a while thereafter, retrains your breath flow as it increases your lung capacity. This is done without special exercises, counting breaths, or learning special techniques. Just get in the habit of holding your fingers in the low-chest position from time to time and reap the benefits.

I did, and here's what happened to me. Not only were my lungs more powerful after doing this (I could sing a note of music and hold that note longer than a trained opera singer), but I became more patient, calmer, steadier on my feet, felt much more comfortable and at ease with my body, could think better and make reasoned decisions easier, was more alert—and became more interested in and motivated by spiritual practices. All this resulted from the simplest of acts, a technique I have taught to thousands of people. Those who committed to the practice reported the same or similar benefits already mentioned.

I have come to regard existence in terms of oneness, manyness, and littleness since my experiences with death. To me, *oneness* is the unity of all things within the reality of the One I still call God, although "God," to my way of thinking, no longer implies male or female, father or mother. *Manyness* is the diversity of ensoulment that God created, for nothing can exist without the imprint of God's fire, that enlivened spark of intelligence and volition. *Littleness* I consider to be you and I as personalities with an ego. I would also include dogs and cats, trees, boulders, and all created things, for each is an entity of purpose and potential. Some of them are more awake and more aware than people who go through their lives as if half-asleep.

Another way of describing this notion of mine follows:

Oneness——unifying factor, the central source of the central vision; **God.**

Manyness——extensions from the central source charged with the outworking of the greater plan; *souls.*

Littleness——expressions of the greater plan; the myriad forms of entities that enable God to experience Itself as Itself through the process of individuation, of birth and death, beginnings and endings; ***individuals.***

∞

I suspect that the Holy Bible, the Koran, the Bhagavad Gita, the To-
rah, and the other sources of inspired revelation are but "memory
books" that reflect, to the degree that they can, our soul's imprinting.
That imprinting also exists within the depths of each one of us, our
heart of hearts, that wellspring of wisdom within. It was shown to me
that we all carry the same imprinting, the same urge to push beyond
what seems to limit us.

Agreements to participate in given embodiments in the earth plane
are made on the soul level before we take on a personality with birth
into flesh and bone. That's why a spiritual or religious commitment in
life is so important. By making such a commitment, we empower ourselves to *remember what we already know*, so that we can be more aware,
have more fun, and live and love more responsibly.

In the Hopi language, the word *family* translates "to breathe together."
Humankind to the Hopi is a single unit with all people members of the
same whole, the same oneness. Science essentially tells us the same
thing: We come from a common ancestry, we are relations, we are one.

10

Bodies and Beings

"God gave each one a cup of day, and from this each one shall mold life."—*Native American saying*

Most of us identify so totally with the face we see in the mirror and the sensations we feel in the body we wear that to entertain any other version of "self" is a real stretch. But let's give it a try anyway. Consider this chapter an exercise in broadening your awareness of visible and invisible bodies and beings.

As a way to understand what I mean when I seek to establish perspective, realize that the term *evolution*, when referring to the soul, describes the ascent of spirit back to its divine source after it has cast aside attachments to the ego body–mind in favor of the truer identity. But the term *involution* depicts the descent of spirit into the world of matter and the taking on of physical form as if "asleep" to the soul's knowledge.

Once the soul is encased in a physical body as the human being we each become, the focus turns entirely to the journey

ahead—and it is a journey, consisting of rites of passage as we grow
through and experience one stage after another in our development.
Typical stages revolve around this patterning:

• the comfort of predictable routines challenged by the excitement
of exploring new options and alternatives;

• enough success to bolster our ego while blinding us to obstacles
that become overwhelming later on;

• invariably losing our bearings and suffering a loss or failure until
we move from ignorance to the recognition that only by being true to
our own authentic self can we ever have real or lasting success and
happiness;

• a sense of well–being and the peace of finding our right place in
the world around us.

Life journeys become sacred journeys once we surrender to our
heart's true desire: God expressing as us through us.

This brings to mind the idea of mission, that sense we all have that
we are here for a reason, a purpose. Caroline Myss, Ph.D., addresses this
issue in her book *Sacred Contracts*.

> **If you look at your life, there are many things you are meant
> to do and many relationships you are meant to have. All of
> them together form what you could call your collective
> Sacred Contract that forms the whole of your life's journey.
> These are really very destined. The general character of this
> planet is very much a place where destiny meets choice. You
> are destined to do certain things in life, and within that
> destiny is choice as to how well, how consciously you will do
> something or you will be in that relationship or you will solve
> the challenges in your life or you will pursue your creativity.**

Myss cautions that our sacred contracts are specifically sculpted to
let us meet our "shadows," whatever is undeveloped, ignored, or misunderstood in our character. In order to be whole, to be all we can be, we
must face the darker part of our nature and heal it.

The main motivators I have noticed that directly affect us in living

∞

are: physical stamina, love, money, and time. As human beings with physical bodies, we are electromagnetic by nature, stuffed full of water and chemicals with a few added minerals. Any change of flux in electrical or magnetic force fields, which either surround us or exist within us, subtly or significantly alters our behavior, emotions, body coordination, and our ability to think and reason coherently. We are easily displaced when environmental impulses do not match those we are used to, and this includes the chemical factor of anything we ingest or absorb. We are like self-contained universes symbiotically connected to and dependent upon the universe at large, yet we are living, breathing transmitters/receivers, multidimensional of scope and limitless in range. We operate more as "nerve cells" than as children of the Most High, until we awaken to the responsibility we have to take charge of our lives and our environment.

I experienced different aspects of breathing and different levels of aliveness in dealing with the aftermath of my near-death episodes. We've already discussed breath. Now I'd like to mention a few things I learned about the immediate and extended packaging we have that is inherent within our aliveness.

Certainly our physical body is set up to breathe air and support our activity in the earth plane. But our physical body is not our only body. We have another one, rarefied of substance, that enables us to equally participate in realms of pure essence, our source place. The air-breathing body is visible. Its spirit counterpart is invisible. Appearing as separate—a physical body and a spirit body—they're both simply differing features of the same energy package that helps us to exist here.

One way I found to understand the basics of our immediate packaging was to realize that we operate continuously through four fields of energy: physical, emotional, mental, and spiritual. This is how I would describe their makeup:

- *Physical*—temperature, odor, electromagnetics, density factors; all of which are measurable scientifically.
- *Emotional*—feelings, sensations, attachments, expressions; all of which are automatically sensed or felt organically.
- *Mental*—thoughts, ideas, perception, memory; all of which

∞

are analyzed and processed intellectually.

• *Spiritual*—insight, wisdom, knowing, creativity; all of which transcend avenues of definability.

Beyond, yet interpenetrating the energy fields that enable us to function as we do, I observed the layers of rarefied substance that make up our spirit body. They were like sheaths or coverings, and they layered the visible body in much the same fashion as onion skin layers around an onion's seed core. Each layer was finer and more subtle than the previous, extending out in refinements of energy or spirit essence from the physical body to a distance that fluctuated according to a person's mood and state of health—from several inches to several yards, or more.

That which can readily be seen is termed the aura and appears as a band of color emanating from the body. Contrary to popular notions, though, the full aura encompasses the totality of the energy fields and layered refinements of spirit that envelope us. Within that totality are myriad stratas of hue, tone, and shape.

As an experiment, ask some friends to come over some evening for aura viewing. Hang a white sheet or use a projector screen as the backdrop and have all the lamps turned down to create subdued lighting. After you've explained the experiment, invite each person to take turns standing with his or her back to the screen while facing the rest of the group, who are standing about ten to twelve feet away. The job of the target individual is to relax. The job of the viewers is to allow their vision to slightly blur as they gaze at but somewhat past the target's features. This is not a contest so there is no hurry. Each person should feel free to report what is seen, if anything, and to engage in dialogue once everyone has had a turn as a target.

The average first timer will feel rather silly doing it and see nothing out of the ordinary; yet, as the evening progresses, usually everyone present will at least have seen a faint band of whitish emanation comprising an inch or two of space around each individual as he or she stood in front of the screen. The rest see bands of color, some more than others. Varying the procedure can lead to fascinating results: have targets mentally project their energy to the left, right, above, or think positive or negative thoughts, etc. Does any of this make a difference in the

∞

aura that can be seen? Does it change its color? Its shape? Reveal something other than an aura?

There's nothing like a personal experience to alter one's opinion about energy fields, spirit substance, and the immediate packaging that seems to define us. Because I have trained so many thousands to do this over the years, I am convinced that just about anyone who wants to can see the "invisible." Admittedly, some individuals are born with the ability, yet the skill can arise suddenly and unexpectedly after a person has undergone a period of intense grief, excitement, or stress, or in conjunction with a spiritually transformative event (regardless of cause).

Our extended packaging has to do with access to and the interrelationships we have with the vastness of the invisible—what some call the paranormal. This includes things like sensing or sighting ghosts and ghostly scenes, apparitions, disincarnates, demons, phantoms, spirit manifestations, nature spirits, strange visuals, bright ones, dark ones, lights of all kinds, guardians, spirit keepers, wee folk, angels, and alien types. We tend to toss anything that exceeds acceptable definitions of reality into the "dustbin of the dubious"—alias, that which is psychic or occult.

Occult means "secret." If you've gone to a newsstand recently, you've seen for yourself that reports about extrasensory perception (ESP), psychic abilities, and psychic phenomena are hardly secret. In truth, psychic abilities are really just enhancements of faculties normal to us—*varied expressions of one mechanism*—that help us to survive and thrive. Such enhancements enrich our lives immeasurably.

Individual learning styles, I discovered, have more to do with how and what a person accesses from the invisible worlds than anything psychic. For instance, auditory learners often hear voices or pick up the easiest on specific sounds or music. Visual learners respond more readily to shape and color, as with symbols, visions, images, and light. Kinesthetic learners can be very touch-oriented and speak of feelings as if sensation itself was their primary language.

To put the idea of extended packaging into some kind of framework, below is a drawing of islands, which illustrates how in the "ocean" of created things, the realm of the invisible (what is below the surface)

extends, supports, and makes possible that which is visible and immediate to our needs (what is on or above the surface).

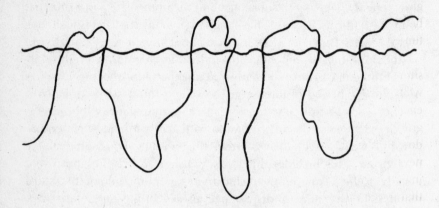

The Physical World:
all that is visible and tangible, the realm of the conscious.

The Astral World:
the invisible reality that supports manifestation,
the realm of the subconscious.

The Spiritual World:
the interconnecting foundation and source of all existence,
the realm of the superconscious.

As a child and during the sixties and seventies as an adult, I was
actively involved in dehaunting houses. I had many encounters with
ghosts, apparitions, lost souls, as well as other types of invisible beings.
There were those who were little more than psychic residue, leftover
energy imprinting from individuals long gone. Sometimes this residue
could be traced to a living person who had simply moved away; sometimes it was connected to a death, as if strong emotions—once expressed—could hang in the air or permeate fabric and wood. On other
occasions, the apparitions appeared and disappeared with a kind of

∞

rhythm, as if they were a recording that was stuck on replay. Some made no response, no change, nothing to indicate the presence of a soul. With others, however, there was a response once they were engaged, and interaction followed (usually rescue work in the sense of helping the individual to realize that he or she was dead and that it was time to move on).

The bulk of my cases during those years, as well as those I engaged in shortly after my near-death episodes, were with fully responsive souls who, for a myriad of reasons, refused to leave the earth plane. One encounter I had was with a six-year-old boy standing at a freshly dug grave. The boy appeared as a living child. I asked him what he was doing there. His audible answer was: "My mommy and daddy told me never to go anywhere without their permission." On further questioning, I learned that he had been hit by a car on his way to school and that it was his body that was buried in the grave. I looked at the headstone and read that the youngster's words were true. I was rather startled at first, then saddened. Try as I may I could not convince him that it was all right to leave the cemetery and go into the realms of God's light. He stubbornly refused to budge without his parents' permission, exhibiting as he spoke the facial expressions and body language of a very determined little boy. I went home and held a prayer service for him, affirming and knowing that whatever was needed to help him would soon occur. The next day I returned to the cemetery and the child was gone.

Over time, I have come to recognize what appears to me as a triune arrangement, a sense of order, to the types of beingness one can find within the layered folds and limitless expanses of the spirit realms. My description of what I have seen follows:

INTRADIMENSIONAL (within levels):

A. *Astral planes.* Middle earth, the muses, fairy folk and wee people, energy beings, ghosts, disincarnates, demons and devils, the hag, emotional discards, passion forms, psychic residue, imprints, futurist manifestations, most abduction accounts (alien or otherwise), psychic creations, enchantments, animal and nature spirits,

∞

guides and guardians, shape shifters, phantoms, lost souls, watchers: *lower kingdoms of ensoulment.*

B. *Inner planes.* Higher beings, ascended masters, spiritual hierarchies, angels, the elders, matrix stewards, spirit keepers, the untarnished soul, access to the great plan: **higher kingdoms of ensoulment.**

INTERDIMENSIONAL (between levels):

Immigrants from other worlds, visitors and travelers from other planes of existence, some aliens, parallels, wind walkers, light workers.

OMNIDIMENSIONAL (beyond dimensional folds and vibratory frequencies):

Abstractions of luminescence; that which is omnipresent, omniscient, omnipotent; the Godhead.

How fast or slow our journey is in life or how many journeys we take, who or what we encounter along the way, how often we encounter them, and at what level depends for the most part on us and the daily choices we make. It's our call. Yet there's a spiritual component, too, a very real one, that overlights creation and every created thing.

11

My Near-Death Research

"The heart has its reasons, which reason knows nothing of."—*Blaise Pascal*

Fate, as I understand it, is fickle. It can be influenced, altered, and shifted around. But destiny is predetermined and cannot be avoided. We can always change the impact of destiny, by the choices we make and how we respond to what occurs. Yet the soul remains ever guided by a greater plan and a higher order. If ever there was proof of this, it is in the testimony of those who have experienced "the other side" of death.

Differing types of people make up this collection of voices: babes being born, toddlers taking their first step, youngsters acting on a dare, teens more interested in a hot date than otherworld journeys, pipe fitters supporting their families, mothers in labor, farmers tilling the soil, health-care professionals who nearly become statistics themselves, mathematicians laboring over a formula, art teachers, stockbrokers, troubled wives, police officers, those caught in the open when lightning strikes. There is nothing else except deathbed visions that gives stronger or more convincing testimony to what may lie beyond death's veil.

A poll taken by *U.S. News & World Report* in March of 1997 estimated that there are fifteen million near-death experiencers in the United States or roughly one-third of those who "died" but later revived. That already high figure does not take into account child experiencers. The best estimate we have for kids who push the envelope of death comes from the work of Melvin Morse, M.D., and his book *Closer to the Light*. He reported the incident rate for youngsters at around 70–75 percent, more than twice as frequent as with the adult population.

The more that medical technology and resuscitation techniques improve, the more there will be people who experience near-death states. And these states are profoundly real, often as disturbing as they are wondrous, always challenging, and ever pushing us as a society to redefine death as well as life.

In light of this, I would like to share with you a brief sampling of some findings from my research on the near-death phenomenon for a quarter of a century.

• Near-death experiences can happen to anyone at any age, even babies in the process of being born (who talk about it once they are verbal). Average length of time without vital signs is between five to twenty minutes. I found a number of people who were able to substantiate that they were "dead" for an hour or two; some revived in the morgue. That the majority come back with little or no brain damage— rather, brain enhancement—is a feature of the phenomenon.

• There are four types of experiences: *initial* (always brief, maybe with one to three elements); *unpleasant or hellish* (more common than admitted); *pleasant or heavenly* (the media favorite); and *transcendent* (seldom personal, focuses more on humankind and creation's story). Scenario elements vary broadly; it is the *patterning* that is universal. Few people experience the so-called classical model (or a tunnel).

• Most experiencers report a greeter who meets them at or before death. Greeters mentioned the most often are loved ones previously dead, angels, light beings, animals (usually beloved pets), and religious figures. Young children occasionally speak of meeting someone still alive (I found one adult who did, too). These living greeters vanish once the experiencer relaxes and are replaced by beings more typical of otherworldly environments. It's as if the main purpose of the greeter (living or deceased) is to relax or alert the individual. Once that occurs, the episode usually shifts into a deeper state (beings of a higher order may then arise).

• Sometimes the greeter is the individual's missing twin. In those cases where a twin was absorbed or aborted during the mother's pregnancy or died soon after birth, this missing one can appear and be at the proper age that he or she should be at the time the living twin faces imminent death. Seldom does the living twin have previous knowledge of the other. Confirmation comes later. The missing twin can also appear in the death scenario of his or her parent.

• On occasion, aborted babies show up as child greeters: to face their mother or father—sometimes in sadness and regret about the abortion, sometimes in forgiveness and reassurance. Child experiencers can meet in death the one or ones who were previously aborted by either parent as well. A relationship can develop between the living child, once he or she revives, and the aborted child. Encounters with the unborn (missing twin or aborted baby) can also include *future* children.

• Amazingly, many experiencers relive their birth as part of their scenario (and accurately, as later checking shows); some, conception. Of those who relived their conception, most were adamant in insisting how the choice was theirs to pick out the genes that would help them have the kind of life that would offer the opportunities they needed for soul growth. Some chose major illnesses or handicaps to accomplish this. A few claimed it was an angel who gave them the gift of a body less than perfect, so that they could learn to be more loving and patient or help others in some special way.

• Energy fields surrounding the physical body are often seen as an aura or glow when the individual departs. Several layers of energy can be described, with the layer closest to the body proper considered the blueprint of the physical. As the individual begins to identify more with the soul than with the personality, this blueprint or spirit body be-

comes the new vehicle. Emotional and spiritual concerns take precedence.

• Experiencer reports describe three different lights that can be
encountered, not just one. A colorless, pulsating radiance or luminosity
that is awesome in its raw piercing power is deemed *primary light* (the
presence of the origin of all origins). A peaceful black depth, sometimes
said to have a velvety tinge of purple to it, shimmers as *dark light* (a
sanctuary of knowingness, healing, and safety). An almost blinding glow
that shines in the range of yellow–gold–white, is *bright light* (the unconditional love of forgiveness and reconciliation). Children, especially, cor-
relate primary light to the one great light of God, with dark light (as
mother light) and bright light (as father light) reflections or aspects of
that Greater Light. All three lights are experienced as intelligent and
communicative and fully alive.

• Readily apparent is that there are various levels to the spirit world
where experiencers go. Consistent patterns portray positive places as
heavens and negative places as hells. Each is more or less desirable than
the next, extending from utter nothingness in the lowest hell to the
bliss of total ecstasy in the highest heaven. Some levels have scenery
similar to the earth plane; others are abstract or foreign looking with
environments than can vary from the grotesque to the sublime. Individuals are drawn vibrationally to whichever place matches the core
essence of the inner development they achieved as a soul living in a
body and having a life in the earth plane.

• Family reunions with those liked as well as those not liked occur
so often in the spirit worlds that such gatherings can be expected.
Grandparents frequently take on the role of guide or guardian. Friends
as well as enemies are important—impressing experiencers with how
any kind of close relationship (positive or negative) can offer a major
opportunity to advance or decline as a soul.

• Religious figures reported more frequently are Jesus, Buddha, Father Abraham, the elders or the Grandfathers (with indigenous and
earth–based cultures), and Lord Yama (god of the underworld in many
Asian societies). Should Jesus or Buddha be seen, they are usually described as joyful and filled with laughter. The opposite is true for Father

Abraham, the elders, the Grandfathers, or Lord Yama, who are often perceived as being stern or serious.

• God or deity is experienced by almost everyone as an all–powerful presence, feeling, or sense. Should God take on form, child experiencers usually see that as a kindly father or grandfather type, always male. Rarely do adults note anything similar, claiming instead that God appeared to them as an immensely brilliant sphere of all-consuming light. Previous religious beliefs or lack thereof makes no difference in how an individual responds to God; yet terminology will differ in accordance with language constraints and cultural stigmas.

• Scenarios can be simple or involved, brief or lengthy. Many are quite personal in content, others concern historical matters or life on other planets in other solar systems. Some people dialogue with the beings met or wind up attending classes in a school or face a tribunal or receive revelations of numerous kinds. The intensity of the episode has a direct bearing on the scenario's impact and the pattern of aftereffects that follow.

• Life reviews can be painful to endure and are occasionally regarded as a type of punishment. These can be experienced as flashes or glimpses of certain life events or viewed as a filmstrip in a theaterlike setting or perceived as a reliving of life from birth to death—including all the consequences of ever having been alive. Invariably, life reviews become strong motivators for change once the individual returns to consciousness or is resuscitated.

• Most experiencers revive with a knowing or having been told that it isn't their time to die, that they have a job to do—a mission yet to perform. Few remember what that job is, even though the existence of a greater plan becomes very real for them, along with the determination to somehow make a positive difference in the world. Many change careers to service–oriented employment or the healing arts.

• When the near–death experience is over, it isn't over. Always there are aftereffects, and these aftereffects are physical as well as psychological. To suggest that such experiences merely alter an individual's attitude ignores the impact and extent of what comes next. Certainly there are those who claim few if any differences afterward; still, nearly 80 percent report that significant if not radical changes occurred. Most of these experiencers said that their aftereffects steadily increased with the passing of time.

• The pattern of aftereffects (mentioned in chapter 9) implies that experiencers can undergo shifts in brain structure, chemistry, and function because of what happened to them, as well as changes to their nervous and digestive systems. Most said they felt as if they had received a power punch or jolt from their experience, as if an energy force of some kind was involved.

• None of the reasons given to explain near–death states—in terms of oxygen deprivation, drug hallucination, temporal lobe seizure, or any other physical or psychological cause—holds up in broad-based research. Neither do such reasons address the entire phenomenon: the experience *plus* the aftereffects.

• Both child and adult experiencers deal with the same pattern of aftereffects, but youngsters tend to have a tougher time because most of them compensate instead of integrate, adjust instead of understand. Children do not have before and after comparisons like adults do, so in describing what happened to them, they often interweave reality in such a way as to diffuse the boundaries between that which is physical and that which is spirit. Because of this, they can imprint to other worlds instead of to this one, causing them to feel foreign or alien as they mature.

• The aftereffects of near–death states are the same or similar to the aftereffects of a transformation of consciousness, no matter how caused. If the impact that transformational episodes can have on people is considered along with how permanent many of the changes can become, a fascinating theory emerges: such events are evolutionary in nature; part of what advances and enriches humankind.

Add to these findings the fact that near–death scenarios hardly ever touch upon what you or I might expect considering the gravity of a person's life choices and deeds. Murderers and mobsters often report episodes so uplifting that they are inspired afterward to make amends for their crimes. Conversely, sterling citizens are those who most frequently report hellish or unpleasant scenarios that leave them in a state of anxiety. Episodes arising from a suicide attempt usually become positive motivators for the individual to accept responsibility for his or her life.

The only sense I could make of this puzzle—and I did find it in every case I investigated—was that whatever the experiencer faced in dying related to whatever he or she had integrated into the deepest self while alive or remained as unfinished business. This had little if anything to do with stated beliefs, but seemed instead to address the growth of that person's soul and what they had yet to learn. Invariably, experiencers would say of their episode, "I got what I needed."

If you really examine the data that emerges from near-death research, my own and others, you begin to recognize something far more dynamic and powerful than the notion that there might be life after death. You recognize that there is no heaven or hell per se, only soul agreements/assignments in an ongoing process of awakening to our true identity in our true "home."

12

The Real Truth About Death

"Whole, he enters the whole. His personal self returns to its radiant, deathless source."—*The Upanishads*

Plato said that philosophy as a discipline is the practice of death. The detachment we gain from cultivating a larger perspective to the fundamental truths of our existence actually prepares us for death.

Facing death means facing our shadow as well as our light, for anything uncomfortable, embarrassing, or painful about the way we have lived and what we have believed surfaces in a way that requires attention. Buddhist teachings describe this as "dying before death": an invitation to empty the mind of everything save the intimacy to be found in a personal relationship with Source. It is an exercise in selflessness, where through forgiveness and compassion our littleness and our manyness can rejoin with the One.

Each and every one of us has an innate knowing about final exits and how to handle them. This is called death wisdom. When we surrender ourselves to a power greater than our own and allow what exists within our deepest self to be remembered, death wisdom heightens and becomes a beacon of strength and courage that we can lean on and be guided by.

An uplifting reminder about the innate knowing we all possess comes from those who have experienced the near–death phenomenon. When I asked the people I had sessions with what death and dying felt like, here's their reply, given as a summary of their collective voices:

HOW IT FEELS TO DIE

Any pain to be suffered comes first. Instinctively and automatically you fight to live. It is inconceivable to the conscious mind that any other reality can possibly exist besides the earth world of matter, bounded by time and space. We are used to living here. We have been trained since birth to live and thrive in the earth plane. We know ourselves to be ourselves by the eternal stimuli we receive. Life tells us who we are and we accept its telling; that, too, is instinctive and automatic.

Your body goes limp. Your heart stops. No more air flows in or out. You lose sight, feeling, and movement, although the ability to hear goes last. Identity ceases. The "you" that you once were becomes only a memory, a dream.

There is no pain at the moment of death. Only peaceful silence. Calm. Quiet. But you still exist.

It is easy not to breathe; easier, in fact, and infinitely more natural.

The biggest surprise for most people in dying is to realize that death does not end life. Whether darkness or light comes next or some kind of event, be it positive, negative, or somewhere in between, expected or unexpected, the biggest surprise of all is to realize you are still you. You can still think; you can still remember; you can still see, hear, move, reason, wonder, feel, question, and tell jokes—if you wish.

You are still alive, very much alive. You are more alive than when you were last born. Only the way of all this is different, different because you no longer wear a dense body to filter and amplify the various sensations you had once regarded as the only valid indicators of what constitutes life. You had always been taught that in order to live you had to wear a body.

If you expect to die when you die, you will be disappointed.

The only thing dying does is help you release, slough off, and discard the "jacket" you once wore (more commonly referred to as a body). When you die, you lose your body. That is all there is to it. Nothing else is lost.

You are not your body. It is just something you wear for a while, because living in the earth plane is infinitely more meaningful and more involved if you are encased in its trappings and subject to its rules.

WHAT DEATH IS

There is a step-up of energy at the moment of death, an increase in speed as if you are suddenly vibrating faster than before.

Using radio as an analogy, this speed-up is comparable to having lived all your life at a certain radio frequency when suddenly someone or something comes along and flips the dial. That flip shifts you to another wavelength. The original frequency where you once existed is still there. It did not change. Everything is still the same as it always was. Only *you* changed, only *you* speeded up or slowed down to allow entry into the next radio frequency up or down the dial.

As is true with all radios and radio stations, there can be bleed overs or distortions of transmission signals due to interference patterns. Normally, most shifts along the dial are fast and efficient; but occasionally one can run into interference, perhaps from a strong emotion, a sense of duty, or a need to fulfill a vow or keep a promise. This interference enables frequencies to coexist for a few seconds, days, or even years.

This may well explain the existence of hauntings and ghosts. But, sooner or later, every vibrational frequency will seek out or be nudged to where it belongs.

You fit your particular spot on the dial by your speed of vibration. You cannot coexist forever where you do not belong. Who can say how many spots there are on the dial or how many frequencies there are to inhabit? No one knows for certain. You shift frequencies in dying. You switch over to life on another wavelength. You are still a spot on the dial, but you move up or down a notch or two.

You don't die when you die. You shift your degree of consciousness and change your speed of vibration. That is all death is. A shift.

I can say without hesitation that you encounter far more than you could possibly imagine when you die. Your previous beliefs do not nec- essarily determine what that is. Life is not as limiting as you may have thought; neither is death. As near as I can tell, there is no end of the discoveries and the encounters you can have beyond death. Truly, death is but a shift in consciousness—like a doorway through which we pass. What we find, no matter what that is, constitutes hardly more than a "wink" in infinity.

The only real death that ever occurs is when a dream we cherish dies.

It has been my experience that our dreams and aspirations in life are what propel and challenge us. People without such dreams meander along with no sense of purpose or meaning; nothing motivates them to change and grow. To have a dream of yourself and your life, and then lose it, that's pain; the kind that rips your heart apart. We can recover, fashion new life from new dreams, but the death of the old one is final. We don't so much resurrect what we think identifies us and makes life worthwhile, as we surrender to God's dream of *who we really are* and live accordingly.

Understanding this is part of death wisdom. In the grace of that wis- dom, we can recognize that our successes and our failures, our laughter and our tears, are but temporary expressions of our soul's urge to expe- rience life through the noisy bodies and soft skin of human form. What lasts, what we carry with us through death and beyond, is the love we have given and received, and the love that we are. If we connect with the wisdom deep within us, that innate knowingness we all have, we would not be so frightened of death nor so attached to life. Reclaiming that wisdom means *listening* to it.

When our granddaughter Myriam died, her parents chose to listen to their hearts rather than to a mortician. In place of a marker to memorialize her, they allowed her organs to be harvested so that others might live; then they established a scholarship in her name to help returning students with the cost of books and tuition (Myriam Renee Huffman Memorial Scholarship at San Jose City College).

In place of funeral, coffin, and grave site, they asserted their right to take care of their dead child "in the way Guidance directed them." Reverently, they arranged for her body to be cremated and named December 22, 1999, as the day for all of us to gather to honor her life and her death. The kitchen table in their small home was turned into an altar of fresh flowers; a single lighted candle welcomed callers who came to pay their respects. What happened next, though, was the sacred made manifest.

North of Santa Cruz, our cars stopped at a place famous among the locals for fresh fish, homemade breads, reasonable prices, and a cozy atmosphere. In place of church pews we gathered around a long table and broke bread together. Some cried. Some visited. All who wished were nourished. When the last vestiges of light embraced a growing darkness, we returned to our cars and followed Kelly and Lydia as they searched for the right place along the California coastline to stop. They chose a wayside park protected by a ring of trees.

Supposedly night had fallen, yet the moon shone with a different, larger, brighter, "in-your-face" kind of light that refused to hide emotions or movements, bushes or paths, or even small rocks from open view. No ordinary full moon, this one was at its perigee, the closest it ever comes to our planet, making the Winter Solstice on December 22 the most spectacular in over six decades. Flashlights were unnecessary as we zigzagged through coastal plant life and dirt trails looking for a spot where we could circle in ceremony around the tiny box of ashes.

Once found, we joined hands. Spirit officiated. When someone was moved to speak, he or she did, taking as much or as little time as feel-ings dictated. Memories of Myriam assumed the status of past tense, as feelings and thoughts surfaced from the deeper reaches of heart and soul. Even Aaron responded, remembering his kid sister in the simple language of child speak.

As if on cue, Kelly, Lydia, and Aaron took up the box of ashes and left the circle. They walked hand in hand the brief distance to the cliff's edge. We watched as the box was opened and hands tossed shadowy clouds of ash skyward, lifted higher still by wind gusts. In a timeless concert of wave-roar, the sea sang Myriam back to God. Whole, she entered the Whole, a radiant, intimate, deathless place that is home to us all.

We made our way back to the picnic area and stood around, sharing tears and hugs. The giant night ball splashed glowing streamers on each person's head and shoulders, on the trees, pavement, picnic tables, cars, plants, trash cans. The wayside stop was transformed into a majesty unmatched by the grandest of cathedrals. No one could have foreseen this: the world around us in praise of light.

Never in the years I have lived have I participated in a ceremony more holy. I realized how far we moderns have drifted away from what makes life worth living: the love we share with each other; the intimacy of touching, caring, and hugging; the value of each person's voice and each person's offering; the simple gestures of togetherness; the willing-ness to help others in service to a higher order. Nothing is more impor-tant than this. Nothing.

Grieving takes a long time. When you lose a child, it takes even longer. The initial stage in the process of grief is one of raw emotion: anger, forgetfulness, rapid speech or none at all, depression, avoidance, guilt, regret, sobbing or bottling up, becoming harder or softer, unex-plained illnesses, obsessive work habits, or the desire to escape, run away, or think only of yourself. All of these responses are typical to the grieving process.

I've noticed, though, that secondary grief sneaks up on you, striking when you least expect it. Just when you accept the loss to the extent that you can and get on with your life, the slightest things can set you

∞

off: seeing a photo of the loved one, glancing at a lookalike in a crowd, hearing a voice, or smelling a fragrance that brings the pain back. This can go on for months, years. During the initial stage people tend to be both numb and reactionary. But the secondary stage is awash in a kind of supersensitivity that is disguised by our best face, the mask we wear to deny our suffering.

Grief in some form can last a lifetime. We don't get over the loss of a loved one as quickly as psychologists say or as depicted in the movies. Yet, we can prolong grief past what is healthy. We can grieve so hard and so often that we hurt ourselves, depress everyone else, and interfere with the soul's passage back to Source.

It is possible to hold on so tightly to the memory of an individual who died that his or her soul can remain "stuck" in the shadowlands at the earth-plane level, unable to progress further into and through the spirit realms. I've seen souls who choose to stick around, however, and for various reasons reappear physically on occasion or project a ghostly image or make themselves known in some manner. Indeed, such an ongoing relationship between the dead and the living can continue for indefinite periods of time. This is not necessarily unhealthy, as it depends on how involved the relationship is. But, should growth and learning be stymied on either end, new experiences blocked out or refused, then both of them (the individual *and* the soul) risk becoming trapped in a false world that benefits neither.

So, what's enough where grieving is concerned? What's too much? Since everyone handles grief and stress differently, standards are usually more harmful than helpful. Turning to a grief counselor or joining a grief group can be an invaluable step toward healing. Yet that quiet space where we can hear our heartbeat and touch the presence of something grander and greater than ourselves is even more valuable. There is much wisdom within us. Prayer and meditation are powerful ways to help us access that wisdom.

Months after Myriam died, Diane, Lydia's mother, told me about something few ever admit yet most people experience: a feeling of exhilaration soon after a loved one's death. She explained: "Alternating between that profound sense of shock, loss, and sadness, I've also sensed an indescribable burst of energy and power. It's almost as if the release of the spirit from the flesh body is accompanied by an energetic release. In my mind's eye I imagine it as a brilliant burst of light, white light, something akin to an atomic explosion—perhaps the energy of fusion."

Diane's portrayal of an energetic shift that is integral to dying included an incredible sense of awe and magnificence, as well as a profound sense of possibility and blessing that she felt at the time. According to her, this exhilaration is the most distinct right after a loved one's death occurs and is fairly dissipated within a couple of weeks. A similar experience follows:

> **Scott Taylor, Minnesota—"A dear friend, Mary Frances, and her six-year-old son Nolan were driving back from a sailing class when she pulled in front of an oncoming car. She died instantly. Early on the fifth morning, Janny, Mary Frances's older sister, and I were alone with Nolan [in the hospital]. We read to him the stories he liked. When I had finished his favorite, Janny put her hand on my arm and with tears in her eyes whispered, 'It's time.' She bent over and whispered in Nolan's ear that it was all right to leave us. She told him that he had been a very brave boy and that it was OK for him to join his mother. We left the room, but in fifteen minutes were summoned back. Nolan's vital signs had taken a sudden turn for the worse. I sat on the window sill, some six feet away. When the beeps declined into an ominous drone, the room filled with the low sobbing of people in grief. But instead of being grief struck, I was in ecstasy. I became lifted up in a joy that defied description. I had just watched a wonderful and precious boy die, and my heart was bursting with a radiance that should have lighted up the room. Gratefully, the family did not see my face or my grin. It was inappropriate."**

The exhilaration people feel when a close friend or loved one dies is very real and very physical, as if something akin to a light flash occurred when the soul took leave of its body.

13

At the Doorway

"These sparks, human souls, which come directly from God, have no end: they are imprinted forever with the stamp of God's beauty."—*Dante Alighieri*

People who sense, feel, or see a light flash released from the body when a person dies are lucky, for it is an awesome thing. I have been privy to such scenes with animals as well. (Although the spirit of most animals is part of a specieswide group soul, some have individuated—especially pets.)

To attend any deathbed is to be present at the altar of the soul. No one should be embarrassed or feel guilty about witnessing the soul's light as it glows in readiness, then flashes off. That flash, at least in what I have observed, is that burst of energy needed by the soul to jettison attachments to the physical body as it frees itself to move elsewhere.

Both science and mysticism attempt explanations for this phenomenon.

∞

Back in the '80s, Janusz Slawinski, a Polish physicist who was a faculty member of the Agricultural University at Wojska Polskiego in Poznan, posited that a *death flash* took place whenever an organism died, including humans. He described this flash as an emission of radiation ten to one thousand times stronger than normal and contained within it was information about the organism that just released it. He was roundly scoffed at by fellow scientists, yet no one has been able to discredit his discovery.

Along this same line, the "jury is still out" concerning the Holy Shroud enshrined in Turin, Italy. This burial cloth is believed to have covered Jesus after His Crucifixion. An *exact* imprint of the man's body it once wrapped appears in both positive/negative formats on the cloth and in such a manner as to reveal details of the individual's death. It is thought that the only way these details could have formed so precisely was through a flash photolysis (the breakdown of materials under the influence of light). In other words, the cloth must have been scorched or seared by an intense emission of radiation coming from the body itself. This implies that Slawinski's death flash might actually be a *light flash*— and that is exactly what is described *when **felt** by an onlooker or relative* (as a sudden upwelling or exhilaration) and *when **seen** by those present* (as an instantaneous burst of light or an unusual glow).

Consider this testimony from Robin McAndrews: "When my husband passed away fifteen years ago, my friend, who was holding my son (then seven months old), myself, and the Catholic priest were in the room. At the moment he took his last breath, the three of us all saw a golden–white light travel in a perfect arc from my husband to explode around our son. Afterward, my friend and I walked the priest to the elevator. We asked him to explain what we'd all just seen. He refused to even comment and shushed me up. What a shame that he couldn't have discussed this! I could have had fifteen years of support rather than the loneliness of being unsure." McAndrews now believes that the arc of light was the final act of a father's love reaching out to protect his son.

An intriguing tidbit is tucked away in the pages of George Meek's book *After We Die, What Then?* that is worth mentioning. He writes that

∞

around the turn of the twentieth century physicians seriously questioned an old religious practice that held that a dead body could not be
violated for three days (in case the departed might want to return and
reclaim his or her former abode of residence). This debate inspired a
physician named McDougall to conduct measurement experiments at
the instant of death. His goal was to see if there was any unexplainable
loss of body weight that might account for the soul leaving the body.
He found that there was, varying between one-half to three-quarters of
an ounce. Five physicians at the Massachusetts hospital later replicated
McDougall's findings. "Such a small package," pondered Meek, until he
realized that sizably smaller crystalline chips could store over
100,000,000 bits of information. Perhaps a half ounce might be limitless.

Our soul, that animating spark of fire that is our core essence, does
not fear death. Only our personality does. The choices we make while
still alive, what we do about what seems to us as true, determines how
close we come to fulfilling our purpose in life—and we each have a
purpose, a reason for being.

When we grieve for another, we're really grieving for ourselves. We
miss the spark of spirit that once animated the person we knew. We
miss what could have been had the individual lived. Death stirs us to
our core, crippling some with unimaginable pain while inspiring others
to search far afield for answers. Why did it happen? What does it mean?
What do we do next? What about the soul?

Few people realize that popular authors—J.R.R. Tolkien in his books
about hobbits and rings of power, C.S. Lewis and his tales of Narnia, and
J.K. Rowling and her Harry Potter series—wrote what they did in an
attempt to explore and come to terms with death. The fantasy worlds
they created enabled them to experience death in a way that they could
face what haunted them without pain. By addressing their own fear,
they opened the door for others to deal with the ultimate in what terrified them, win out over that fear, and emerge triumphant. Considering
how many millions have bought their books, their personal quests for
understanding have come to depict humankind itself in its larger quest
to solve the sacred mysteries of life and death. All three authors designed their stories for children and the child in all of us. All three used

supernatural drama so effectively that what happens to the characters happens to us. We relate to the stories because of how our soul's memory is stimulated.

Many who are frightened by these books are actually frightened of death.

Rings, wardrobes, and magic wands aside, it never ceases to amaze me how deft people are at avoiding the subject of death or how panicky they get should mention be made of anything having to do with the "psychic" or the "intuitive." Unfortunately, neither happenstance nor coincidence explains the unexplainable.

After decades of experimentation, I discovered that our psychic/intuitive sense—and, yes, we all have it—is simply one of many survival skills we share as human beings, a particular skill that enables us to negotiate the uncertainties of life more easily. Intuition, just as with the intellect, improves with usage and training; yet no one, even today, can identify exactly how it operates. Some say intuition is the language of the heart. I view it, though, as a perceptual enhancement, an interface between our energy and the energy around us, that, like a thermostat, provides a readout on present and changing conditions, varied options, and futuristic alternatives. Should we ignore or misinterpret the readings it gives, that same information will tend to interweave the symbolic structure of our dream state. To deny the existence of our intuitive nature is to deny what makes us human—our instinctual need to interrelate with one another and connect in a higher, more compassionate manner.

Our intuitive sense kicks into high gear when death threatens or if someone important to us passes through death's door. Any message about this death usually appears in our dream states or through a sudden shift in our behavior that seems to be directed or guided by spirit. Here are a few examples:

> *Stephanie Wiltse, New York*—"After my father had been admitted to the hospital with a stroke, I awakened from a dream about him every morning at exactly 5:30 a.m. The last morning, and third dream, I dreamt that my father was being wheeled out of an insane asylum (he had indeed been

mentally impaired for some time). I was aghast that he was being released. But when I protested, I found myself chased around the facility as if I had been mistaken for an inmate. I awakened with a chuckle, thinking how ironic it was that he would escape whilst I would be confined there. Later that morning word came that my father had died. The time of death was 5:30 a.m.!"

Susan Barreto, New York—"My son Jordon, who had just moved to Rome, Italy, died in his sleep. No cause of death was found. My most spiritual friend Julia, who had been close to Jordon since he was two, called me about a very real dream she had. She was in a beautiful house in mountains covered with snow. She had a feeling that a little kid was nearby and she heard, 'Aunt Julia, Aunt Julia.' She looked down and saw a beautiful pair of Italian shoes, then her gaze followed up the body until she was staring into Jordon's eyes. Jordon told her he had made a conscious choice to leave, as he had the opportunity to partake in something but he had to leave to do it. She said that the acne on his face was gone, she could feel him breathe, and she could also smell him. They walked outside and Jordon disappeared, then she woke up. Jordon's brother, Carlos, was upset that Jordon hadn't come to see him, and then he had a dream in which Julia took him to the same house as before and there was Jordon. They sat at the kitchen table and Carlos asked Jordon to give him a hug. He did. Carlos woke up crying."

Cynthia Sue Larson, northern California—"I went on vacation to Canada with one of my dearest friends and our spouses, and we got to talking about our wishes for funerals. John, the husband of my friend, insisted that he didn't want his wife, me, or anyone else to be sad and depressed when he died. He said he'd much prefer that everyone enjoy a grand celebration to remember him and how much he loved us. This idea sounded great, so I promised John that I would do my best to celebrate when he died. Many years passed. On the very day that John was to die, I inexplicably felt compelled to prepare an 'unbirthday party.' This urge came over me as I was shopping with my daughter at an art supply store, and she asked for a toy that looked like a fish and wrote like a pen. Unlike me, I said, 'Why not?' I then proceeded to buy another toy pen for my other daughter and explained that these were unbirthday presents for the party we would have that very evening. My husband baked a cake. I frosted and decorated it. We all enjoyed the unique celebration. Afterward, I took a nice hot bath. While in the tub I got a phone call from John's wife at the hospital telling me that John had just died. I felt amazed that I had kept my promise *as* he was actually dying."

Have you ever noticed that the various kingdoms of nature respond to our life's passages as well? Shooting stars, a dog's howl, birds crashing into windows, weather oddities, a favorite mirror cracking or a clock stopping—all take on a heightened significance if associated with the moment of someone's last breath. It's as if the natural world participates in message giving, either as a warning of what's to come or for comfort and reassurance after a person's death has occurred.

It is true that a person can "die" long before his or her body does, even years before. Advance departures such as these usually leave the body operating as if on automatic pilot, devoid of the creative spark that enlivens life: eyes vacant, face blank, chatter mindless, routines dulled. You get the feeling being around someone like this that "no one is home"—the body is empty. This vacancy can be temporary, however, as the soul is quite capable of leaving its body and coming back at will. Unbearable pain is often the reason for "exits"; pain relief, for "returns." Should the soul remain away, the body can revert to the consciousness of a small child and eventually wither or wear out.

For the majority, passages through the doorway of death are usually smooth, easy, and unobstructed, coinciding with the merger of soul and personality and the body's demise. Interestingly, hospice statistics show that folks who cling to life, defying all odds about when they might make their transition, often leave rapidly and as if part of a single group once the weather changes and there is a sudden drop in barometer and temperature readings. Also, more people die during the morning hours than at any other time of day, especially on Mondays.

Our earthly bodies are strongly influenced by earth laws and the energy tides that ripple and spin throughout the airspace of earth. I believe that death itself is a physical force, not just a condition that describes the absence of breath and pulse beat. Powers of greater import affect the force it wields, but so too does the prevailing mindset of the dying individual and his or her significant others. Because of this, a promise or concern can delay the finality of death. I've seen this happen on many occasions.

During the time I lived in Boise, Idaho, Margaret Matthews, a dear friend of mine, was killed in a horrible accident. Margaret, her husband, Frank, and their grandson were traveling by car to Yellowstone Park for a vacation. He was driving; she was on the passenger side, and their grandson was wedged in between them. Just as they crossed a bridge, a pickup truck, driven by a drunken teen showing off for his girlfriend, slammed head-on into them. Margaret was decapitated. Frank was crushed, yet he stubbornly clung to life as he and his grandson were rushed to the nearest hospital. When the attending physician determined that only the boy's pelvis had been broken and that he would recover, Frank drew a sigh of relief and promptly died. Even when mangled beyond belief, he was protective of his grandson and would not leave until he knew for certain that the boy would live.

The death of Margaret and Frank Matthews was a triple tragedy. Once their grown children were notified, they in turn broke the news to Frank's elderly mother, their grandmother. She was so shocked, she died instantly. As it happened, at Margaret's request, my former husband and I were in the Matthews's home early that evening holding a Search for God Study Group meeting (spiritual studies taken from the readings of the late Edgar Cayce). Their son telephoned, surprised that anyone was there, and we talked at length. The meeting became a prayer circle where each person in attendance served as a guide to assist the three souls in making their transition into God's great light and to help the grandson.

I tell you this because of what happened next. While making certain that there was plenty of food for everyone at the Matthews's home during the days before the funeral for all three, I also did door duty. That means I was standing at the threshold when the neighbor across the street came running toward me, screaming at the top of her lungs, "Margaret can't be dead. Tell me she's not dead. I saw her and I talked to her when the sheriff's deputy said she had died. That's not possible. She was here and I talked to her." All of us did a double take and gathered around.

The woman's story, told with utter conviction and backed up by the deputy's log of her telephone call, went like this: She was outside sweeping her stoop when she looked up and saw Margaret walking along her front sidewalk. She yelled at her and asked how she was doing. Margaret stopped, faced the woman, smiled, and said she was just fine. She smiled again, turned around, and kept walking to the door, unlocked it, and disappeared inside as the door closed. The neighbor thought nothing of this exchange until, after finishing her chores, she turned on the radio in her kitchen and heard the bulletin. She called the sheriff's department to see if the broadcast was a prank and learned, much to her shock, that the time she and Margaret had been visiting *was the exact same moment Margaret was killed.*

I asked the neighbor if she had ever before experienced anything supernatural. She said no, then she stunned the crowd that had gathered by saying: "A couple of weeks ago, Margaret and I were talking, and I told her that I wanted more than anything else in the world to know if there was life after death. She promised me that the proof I needed would soon be coming. Then she smiled that special smile of hers, just like she did when I saw her yesterday."

This isn't all that Margaret did after her death. She manifested countless times, always seen as fully alive and responsive, whenever she could help another or be of service. These appearances of hers, plus other types of after–death communications from her, went on for almost a year. Seven years later she reappeared to fulfill a prediction she had once made to me: that when I enrolled in a certain class on the power of affirmative prayer, I would look up and see one of her daughters looking back at me. That did happen, even though her family and I had not communicated since the funeral. Several class members saw Margaret in the room before I did, then the lights went out. They did not come back on until Margaret's presence was acknowledged.

Can the dead return after they die?

You bet they can.

For a period of time after death, it is commonplace for the dearly departed to return home or stick around that which is familiar. Unfinished business draws them back, or simply the desire to let their loved ones know they're okay. Once satisfied that they have done all they can for the living, most of them complete their transition into the spirit realms.

Incidents do occur, however, in which the dying do not merge with their soul but remain a disembodied ego floating around or simply existing until someone or some thing wakes them up. That's why prayer is so important at the deathbed and afterward. As powerful as the soul is, its memory can cloud or at times seem forgetful. Even a soul can use a little help.

14

Sharing Crossover

"Yes, there is such a thing as a good death. We ourselves are responsible for the way we die. We have to choose between clinging to life in such a way that death becomes nothing but a failure, or letting go of life in freedom so that we can be given to others as a source of hope."—Henri J.M. Nouwen

When we think of the deathbed, most of us envision a sterile place: a hospital bed, whispers, fear, muffled crying, tubes sticking out, machinery bleeping, frustration, suffering, and the inevitable "weight" of silence. No place is more solemn or to many, more dreadful.

I invite you to rethink your vision of the deathbed.

Not everyone can or should do what Kelly and Lydia did with their daughter. Yet all of us have much more power than we realize to alter and rearrange the circumstances of an individual's final moments. We can even personally participate in helping that person move through death's threshold, during the body's actual passage, with an exercise called empathic experiences. Make certain first that you have the permission of those involved before any action is taken, as the freedom to choose must always be respected. If there is agreement, then reclaim the power of the deathbed by reconnecting death with life.

Our comings and goings are not done in random bits and pieces. Life and death are a single continuum, a flowing stream of feeling and thought. Fear becomes fearsome when we try to divide or separate one part of a person's life from the other parts. Honoring the whole continuum returns the power to where it belongs: the individual. So, bring in family and friends. Music. Pleasant smells. Laughter. Poetry. Maybe a wiggly puppy. Children. Sounds. To the extent that the one who is dying can handle it, enliven the place.

When my Uncle Julius died, four of his sisters sat on or around his hospital bed and engaged with him in a rousing discussion of current events, especially those that concerned the situation of China taking back Hong Kong. In full voice Julius predicted that the people of Hong Kong would lose much of their freedom when this happened. Pleased that he had contributed to the topic at hand, he died. Quickly. Easily. He died as he had lived, an adept seer of the political and financial scene, surrounded by his loved ones who enjoyed a good debate as much as he.

Have you ever thought of singing your loved one out? The occasions where I know this was done involved family and friends joining hands and then circling around the one who lay dying. In unison or taking turns with single offerings, they sang, and the music kept flowing until the dying individual breathed for the last time. Pain and sorrow quickly dissipated afterward, for what the people really shared was the sound of the soul's breath—the music of love.

Our brain is wired for music, especially for perfect fifth and fourth musical intervals. Clinical evidence suggests that the regions for music, math, and intelligence are interrelated within the brain. Music itself can influence our physical behavior and determine how satisfied and contented we are. For instance, you can literally control a person's nervous system and basic response patterns—respiratory, circulatory, and metabolic systems—by the rhythm, tempo, and pitch of music. That is why food markets play slow "elevator" music in their stores (so you'll linger and buy more), and fast food eateries feature lively pieces (so you'll eat quick and run, which creates rapid turnover and improves profit).

There's a science to music that has been known and utilized in some fashion for thousands of years. In medieval times, for example, just as there were midwives for birth there were midwives for death. Death midwifery was usually practiced in chambers where the playing of special harp music aided the dying in making their transition, surrounded by an atmosphere of compassion and grace. Much pain and suffering were alleviated in this manner.

Therese Schroeder–Sheker revived the ancient practice of death midwifery and made it her life's work by initiating the first school in the nation that teaches prescriptive music, a special type of music that a physician can prescribe for the dying, in addition to or in place of drugs. This two–year study and clinical internship program is affiliated with St. Patrick Hospital in Missoula, Montana, under the auspices of the Chalice of Repose. People train there to learn a uniquely beneficial way to offer unconditional loving care for those who are about to die. Termed music thanatology, the music played is not patterned on the order of a concert but consists, instead, of deeply spiritual and loving sounds delivered by practitioners who work in teams and position themselves and their harps on either side of the dying patient. The vigil they keep is individualized to the patient's needs for facilitating the unbinding process that is central to a conscious, peaceful, or blessed death. Unbinding is where we, in the truth of our genuine self, allow our spirit body to loosen its connections to the physical body and float free. No pretense. No holding on.

Music thanatology is so effective that not only is the dying patient able to let go of the earth plane supported on the wings of love, but the families as well as the health–care givers are equally healed and helped. It is my dream that in the near future every state in the nation, and maybe every country, will offer training either as part of or patterned after what is available through the Chalice of Repose and that the choice to have this type of loving care at death will be a possibility for every person.

Other sources exist for using music at the deathbed. Gilles Bedard, a

∞

French and English speaker from Montreal, Quebec, and a near-death experiencer, has initiated "Music from the Dawn of Light." His program is based on a collection of contemplative music, chosen to convey a deep sense of sacredness and reverence. He emphasizes how important it is for hospice workers and health-care providers to learn how to use this type of music with their patients. To that end, he offers a series of workshops for professionals, a quarterly newsletter on the latest releases appropriate for the dying, plus a general list of recommendations. Considering the growing demand for beneficial yet inexpensive ways to help the dying experience a good death, Bedard's project is becoming an invaluable resource.

As death approaches, what was once considered insignificant is exaggerated in importance. A card, a phone call, a flower, a comb gliding through hair, a gentle massage, a pat on the hand—this and more, the simplest of acts—make the growing sense of emptiness easier to bear. No one is exempt from that emptiness, even people of deep faith. It's part of endings. It's one more step during the preparation to let go, to unbind spirit from matter.

You and I, any and every one, can make an important and invaluable contribution in the process of dying. We can share in the actual crossover. We can coparticipate in the spiritual dimensions of a person's death, either as part of a spontaneous incident or through an exercise called empathic experiences.

Empathic experiences are where two or more join together in consciousness and feeling to share in the act of dying. These sessions are heartfelt and consist of the person who remains "becoming one with" or "participating in" or "witnessing fully" both internal and external aspects of the death event as it actually happens to the individual who is leaving. Although initially this exercise may seem little more than a standard visualization routine, I assure you that once the session begins, anything superficial or fanciful is replaced by a quality of absolute realness.

Empathic experiences, if sincerely engaged in, can directly align those involved with soul-level energy—creating a rare opportunity for true spiritual intimacy.

∞

An example of an empathic experience that occurred spontaneously concerns a woman who began to hear soft melodious music as she maintained a vigil next to her dying brother. She looked around to see if a radio was on, and, as she did, a brilliant light filled the room (the light flash). She turned just in time to see her comatose brother open his eyes, smile, and raise his arms upward. Then, "As real as anything I've ever seen, a being of light reached out and took my brother by his wrists and pulled. My brother's spirit popped right out of his physical body—snap—just like that. I was so surprised, I jumped." With eyes wide open, the woman witnessed the being of light and her brother (now in spirit) float out of the hospital room through a mistlike archway that had formed in a nearby ceiling corner. A scent of roses permeated the air where the discarded body shell lay.

Another of my cases was a woman who saw a murder happen in broad daylight on a busy street in Russia. As the assailant ran, she rushed to help the one who was stabbed, but before she could begin emergency measures, she found herself suddenly unable to move. Instantly she joined in consciousness with the dying individual and empathically shared the victim's life review from birth to death, as well as the spirit's crossing to "the other side."

Then there's the incident in England of a woman who saw and felt every aspect of her husband's death as he died, as if she were his proxy. And a young man in Texas whose dead parents came to visit him shortly after they were murdered, as he himself lay dying of an illness. Their appearance and what they told him was so comforting that against all odds he revived, totally transformed.

No one planned to have the empathic experiences I mentioned. They simply happened. Yet wonderful miracles such as these can be *invited* and *caused*. We can return the deathbed to what it once was, the province of family and friends and those with an open heart who choose to support the dying process by aiding their loved one in every possible manner.

I would like to share with you what I've seen others do and what I have done myself regarding three ways that empathic experiences can occur. [The following instructions originally appeared in my book *The*

∞

Complete Idiot's Guide to Near-Death Experiences (with David Morgan). I want
to thank Macmillan/Pearson for giving me permission to quote from
this material.]

1. *Accidental Empathic Experiences.* As with the woman and her dying
   brother, the actual moment of death is unpredictable. If you're not
   alert, you could miss it. What might prepare you is to know the
   common precursor signals, such as the suddenness of soft music when
   nothing is playing, a pleasant smell that cannot be associated with
   anything nearby, a light that mysteriously brightens, a glow that
   appears around the dying person, changes in his or her behavior
   that indicate a heightening of awareness, and the sensing or feeling
   of an unseen presence. Should any of these incidents occur, immediately look straight at the dying individual and allow your vision
   to diffuse (as if you were looking slightly past him or her). Relax.
   Wait. You may sense more than you see.

2. *Invited Empathic Experiences.* This involves knowing about the "signals"
   just presented (clues that alert you to what may soon occur) and
   having the willingness to relax, wait patiently, and be open and
   receptive. More important, though, is intention. Your desire to be an
   active participant needs to be admitted and prearranged, either with
   the one about to die, if that person is capable of communicating, or
   with the family. Once the appropriateness of your being there has
   been established, I recommend that you—

   • Consider your role as being that of a helper.
   • Communicate this to the dying individual either verbally or tele-
     pathically (a mind-to-mind connection made through the pro-
     cess of thinking and feeling it so).
   • Hold his or her hand, if possible, or touch in some other appro-
     priate way.
   • Verbally and telepathically reassure the individual that it's OK to
     "leave."
   • Be aware of and alert to your own feelings and inner promptings.

∞

- If it feels right to do so, within your mind's eye "see" yourself "walking" him or her into the Light.
- Allow subjective imagery to arrange itself by itself. Don't assume.
- Withhold any tendency to force or control the situation or to go farther than the initial entry into the other worlds.
- Offer a prayer or some form of positive upliftment/protection.
- Share on whatever level feels right, then fully release; let go either by saying the words, or thinking or feeling that the individual is gone.

3. *Preplanned and Guided Empathic Experiences.* Empathic experiences that involve a guided visualization exercise prepare the one about to die for the death event. All parties concerned need to agree to this preparatory exercise in advance. You must be comfortable with your role as a guide—relaxed, respectful, and in a spiritual state of mind. Prayer or some form of positive upliftment/protection is helpful at the start. The visualization itself incorporates the basic elements of the near-death phenomenon as a pattern. This is done verbally and as follows:

- ◆ Pace your breathing with that of the dying individual. Should his or her breathing be erratic, your own steady breaths are usually enough to bring calm.
- ◆ Talk softly, saying that the individual is now leaving his or her body and floating upward. Speak of how easy and effortless this is, and how good it is to leave the heaviness and the pain of the physical body behind.
- ◆ Acknowledge the gathering of simple shapes and forms in the airspace around both of you. Dark or light makes no difference. Just note that something is coming together. The person's body may still be visible as his or her attention shifts to whatever seems to be forming midair. Encourage this shift in attention, as you—

- Affirm the presence of a special light that is slowly growing

∞

brighter and brighter, but does not hurt the eyes to see.

- Mention that any sudden sense of speed is OK, that it's all right to go faster and faster, maybe even to feel a wind brushing your face.
- Prepare the individual for a stop and an increase in light, and for the presence of strangely familiar, melodious music and sweet smells.
- Assure the individual that it's OK to greet those who might appear, be they a loved one, an angel, a light being, a religious figure, a pet, or some other type of animal.
- Encourage engagement between them: talking, dialogue, a question-and-answer session, or whatever the individual might feel drawn to do.
- Remain in this state for a while, then return as you came—the two of you—back to earth, back to your separate bodies.
- Linger with the feeling of being back, as you continue to talk softly to the individual in a gentle way until he or she opens both eyes or you sense sleep has come. The session is over.

Should you use this type of guided visualization or something akin to it, remember to invoke all the faculties. I have found that the deeper you get into this, the more feelings and sensations and emotions you can describe and invite, the more successful the dying individual will be in accepting what is about to occur. Once may be enough for this exercise, or several sessions may be desired. If the eyes are open or closed really doesn't matter since the intensity of desire is there. Also if the imagery is vivid, it does not make any difference whether the dying individual is conscious, asleep, or comatose. Research has shown that the brain can still register what you say and, in most cases, follow along.

Empathic experiences, like any other near-death-like state, can be life changing for those involved. The depth of intimacy and core spirituality that can be accessed in doing them is extraordinarily rich. Whether done as part of a religious ritual or in an act of love and support, empathic experiences often mimic or duplicate what is known about physical death and the moment of crossing over.

∞

Reports from people who coparticipate in such events are on the rise. Surprising is the large number who claim to have coexperienced the entirety of a dying person's life review and later are able to testify to details in that review that they could not possibly have known previously. Credit for this amazing phenomenon is given primarily to the hospice movement's emphasis on stay–at–home care for the terminally ill. I rather suspect, however, that the real reason for the substantial increase in things of the spirit surrounding crossover is that the public is finally willing to listen to their heart instead of to the experts, and to be more open and receptive, *allowing rather than controlling.*

I received a telephone call a few years ago that illustrates this change of preference. It was from a young man in New York City who was dying of AIDS. He insisted that I tell him what I know about death. My reply noted a long list of experts in the field whose work I could recommend. "I already contacted every one of them," he countered, "and none of them talk about death. You've already died. Tell me, what was it like?" I spent nearly an hour with him. What was shared between us inspired my recording of *As You Die* (available now in several formats; refer to later in this book for details).

As You Die is designed to be played at the deathbed: to help with ideas and suggestions during the preparatory stage; to talk the one who is dying through death as it physically occurs; and, for about ten to fifteen minutes after the cessation of breath, to support crossover when the soul breaks free of connections and leaves.

As You Die is my way of being there, of doing what I can to assist the dying. Those left behind benefit, too, for the material on the tape and on the video helps them in coming to terms with their own sense of loss.

15

Healing Helpers

"Between the people of eternity and the people of the earth there is constant communication."—*Kahlil Gibran*

You can't tell a person who has just lost a loved one that death isn't real. It *is* real, it is physical, and it's messy. When death comes, it's as though the lights go out, as if someone or something unplugged a plug in a socket and suddenly the energy that had once animated the individual is no more.

Have you ever watched a person die? The extremities go numb, the body organs fail in domino fashion, and the head, in most cases, dies from the back forward as one would pull a cap over the head and down the face. Skin tone grays to a colorless paste. Body openings ooze. There is a loud death rattle like a deep throaty "arrgh" as the body jerks, then collapses. The shell that remains begins to cool as emptiness spreads a cloak of silence.

There is usually an odor, such as musk or after-shave, perfumelike fragrances, the scent of roses, or even noxious smells.

∞

Why odor? Perhaps escaping body gasses may explain the smells, yet maybe not. There are many mystical legends and religious traditions that claim that a departing soul will give off a smell that corresponds to the degree of spiritual development attained while an ego personality on earth. The higher the development, the sweeter the smell; if saintly, there is the scent of roses.

If your belief system restricts your sense of identity to the confines of your physical body, I have noticed that death then becomes *the enemy*, robber of love and companionship, destroyer of time's cradle of opportunity. But if you recognize that all of us are more than our bodies (and we are), death becomes instead *the shape shifter*, guardian of spirit's journey through physical matter, restorer of vision and truth.

Death forces us to really see, to feel and hear as never before. Our experience of reality alters as it nears. The aura surrounding the dying person's body changes. Visitors come (spirit beings whose job it is to prepare the dying for the crossover).

Hours or days before most people die and in advance of the light flash, I have seen that the aura grays into nothingness as the creative spark dulls. This shift in the energy field coloration has been especially noticeable to me with those who exhibit no cause for alarm (like people entering an elevator or seating themselves aboard a public conveyance) or when surgery approaches or when the illness they have does not appear to be life threatening. This graying or absence of the aura is such a reliable signal either of trouble afoot or that death awaits that I snap to attention whenever I recognize it. I always ask in prayer for guidance on what action to take in situations like these. Sometimes I'm directed to stay and help; other times to give a warning or to avert my eyes and silently walk away. Over the years I have learned to respect the soul's will, hidden or revealed, as I know there is a higher order to what seems apparent. Judgment is not mine to have; faith is.

The coming of visitors is as reliable a signal that death is near as are changes in one's aura. For instance, heavenly beings appeared to my sister, Judy, when she was faced a while ago with having to undergo open-heart surgery to replace a faulty heart value. That is how she knew how grave her situation was and that she had best get her affairs in order. She had no fear, just a knowing.

Judy is a longtime nurse, an expert in her field of health care, who has dedicated herself to continual learning. She is also a good listener and tells numerous stories about the deathbed visitations her patients have had and about the spirit communications which the living regularly receive whenever they are quite worried or in great need.

"You can expect this," she explained. "It's a sign that things are serious. And these contacts, they're real. I've checked on many of them and what people were told. Always they check out. I *know* what an hallucination is, and these aren't hallucinations. Patients' descriptions are clear, coherent, accurate. They do not act confused when this happens, nor does their speech meander. If a person isn't that seriously ill or in crisis, you don't hear about these spirit visitors. So, when it happened to me, I knew exactly what was going on and what it meant."

Judy suffered the worst pain she had ever experienced from the surgery. She has a deeper compassion for people who undergo similar operations because of it. "Open-heart procedures have become so routine that doctors seldom acknowledge what their patients go through. And they flatly ignore the spiritual side of life and any patient's report about messages from the spirit world."

Judy is typical of every nurse I have ever met who is willing to talk about the otherworldly communications that patients have received. These professionals are convinced such occurrences are real. A director of nurses at a large hospital once told me: "There's a spiritual realm and it's all around us. If we don't admit this and listen to our patients' stories without judgment, we aren't doing our job."

Another nurse active in the healing arts who truly listens is Christina Moon of Arkansas. "As a hospice nurse, I am often at the bedside of dying patients. Sometime ago I became aware of an angel who is with me. This angel's name is Rab'ai. The angel is huge, and the angel is black. It's the softest, gentlest black that one could imagine. It's quite indescribable, really. Just feels like one enters it and joins with it in the most sacred of ways, fully nurtured and cared for within this darkness. I became aware that the wings of this angel emerge from between my own shoulders, as if we have become one. At these times, I feel the

∞

wings (huge) come forward and cradle the dying one in their feathered tips. It's the most wondrous experience. It almost brings me to my knees to be blessed with this companion's presence within and alongside me."

Moon's experience with a patient named Jill is illustrative of how a soul can leave the body: "She made a few reflexive gurgling sounds in her throat. There was a long pause and then, with my left hand on top of her head, I felt that last thrust of the spirit exiting her body. It felt just like a tension in her head, a tightening, a pushing, a last letting go. And she was out of her body. There were times when I had one hand on the top of Jill's head and the other on Sophie's back. (Sophie is Jill's daughter.) At these times, I felt like an energetic bridge between the two, mother and daughter." Incidentally, Rab'ai was present when this incident occurred, as a healing helper from the spirit worlds assisting Moon in her work.

Christina Moon's experiences are not unique. Health–care providers of every persuasion, including doctors, are "coming out of the closet" in increasing numbers and admitting the extent to which they pray for their patients, see the aura, and engage with spirit beings for assistance in administering the right treatment in the right manner. Chief among these professionals is trauma physician Michael Abrams, author of *The Evolution Angel*.

Not only is the health–care field waking up to the help readily available to them from "the other side," but so is the average individual. We all have equal access to that font of higher wisdom and love through dreams and visions, prayer, tuning in directly, and by request. We all have the same ability to pass on what we receive, along with the loving light we already possess, by becoming healing helpers ourselves.

A way that we can do this at the deathbed is through the power of breath used as a specific breath routine. Called co–meditation, the routine is a godsend in how it enables people to bond in spirit and breath and essence. I first heard of it from Richard W. Boerstler, Ph.D., a psychotherapist who uses holistic and meditative approaches in his work with the terminally ill. He wrote a small book about the procedure called *Letting Go*.

Essentially, co–meditation involves two individuals, a helper and the one about to die, agreeing to breathe together. The helper explains the technique, asking for the other's close attention, in terms something like this:

- With eyes opened or closed, make the sound of "AH" on an out-breath and stretch the "AH" out until it becomes AAAAAAAAAHHHHHHHHHH.
- Thinking is not necessary. Drop everything from your mind.
- If you want to think of something, just focus on a pleasing image in your mind's eye, perhaps a scene from nature.
- No thoughts allowed. Just the image.
- Relax, breathe in as you would normally do, then breathe out with a long AAAAAAAAAHHHHHHHHHH.
- Synchronize breaths together.

Both the helper and the dying do this in unison, breathing in and out, with an "AH" on the out-breath—just the "AH" as you breathe out, just the letting-go sound—for "AH" is the sound of release. Relax and listen. Listen to each other, and listen to your own breath.

Throughout the session, the helper keeps his or her eyes on the lower chest area of the one who is dying, watching any movement, joining in the "dance" that death makes. Sometimes the helper makes a comment during exhalation; perhaps one of these:

> *The sound of my voice is like music.*
> *The song I sing is of peace, sweet peace.*
> *Now is the time of letting go.*

If the individual about to die is breathing too rapidly, the "AH" technique is inappropriate. Then counting breaths should be used in place of the "AH" breath, even if that means only the helper is doing the counting. The goal is to calm the dying individual by sharing the most powerful movement any human being engages in: breathing. Twenty- to thirty-minute sessions are long enough at any given time. Do them as often as agreed upon.

It is encouraging to see how much pain and anxiety is relieved

∞

through this simple, easy procedure. Anyone can be the helper. This means loved ones can actively participate at the deathbed; *they can do something*, instead of fretting, staring into space, reading a magazine, being upset or frightened, worrying, or feeling left out.

The awareness, needs, and language of the one about to die will change the closer he or she comes to that last breath. We must make allowance for this. Nonsensical gestures and words couched in symbolic story form tend to predominate. For the majority this has nothing to do with drugs or hallucinations, but is rather a form of language unique to the deathbed, regardless of cultural tradition. It's as if the act of dying automatically switches brain hemisphere function to what is called our right brain (that subconscious, creative, dreamy part of our nature that ever seeks for meaning and wholeness). This doesn't imply that individuals lose lucidity and logic as their days wane. It just indicates that *dreaming tends to become a wide-awake, conscious activity* that influences how they speak (including any conversations and interactions they might have with visitors). One book will teach you all you need to know about how to understand the language changes that occur with the dying and how to communicate with them more effectively. That book is *Final Gifts*, written by hospice nurses Maggie Callanan and Patricia Kelley.

Having said this, I want to further clarify that a person's mind can remain lively throughout the death process and crossover (as with my Uncle Julius).

Of interest in this regard is research that made newspaper headlines in early July of 2001. It concerned a British scientist who examined heart attack patients and found evidence which suggests that consciousness may continue even after the brain has stopped functioning and the patient is clinically dead. Sam Parnia, one of two doctors from Southampton General Hospital in England, had been studying the near-death experience and discovered that people with no brain function can still have well-structured, lucid thoughts with reasoning and memory formation during the time they have flatlined. Parnia is quoted as saying: "We need to do much larger studies, but the possibility is certainly here to suggest that consciousness, or the soul, keeps thinking and reasoning even if a person's heart has stopped, he is not breathing, and his brain activity is nil."

The coming of death is far more complex and varied than any platitude can address. How the final moment is experienced by the one who is dying cannot be predicted. To promise anyone a certain outcome betrays the integrity of the brotherhood and sisterhood we share as members of the same human family. We can offer ideas and suggestions, give personal or religious testimony about death, but what follows that last breath is intimate to the one involved.

We do not program that final moment; we *allow*. And we can do this by affirming God's mercy and God's love, or whatever else represents to you the highest possible good.

It is said that to die in a state of sincere and deep prayer or while supported by the loving prayers of others is the greatest protection anyone can have at crossover, and the best way to ready ourselves for spirit life. I have found this to be true. I have also discovered that there is more that our churches and spiritual groups can do in regard to the power prayer has; they can form teams of Healing Helpers.

Healing Helper teams consist of volunteers from the assemblage who have agreed to come forward to the podium or central space at the close of worship ceremonies to serve anyone's needs by praying with him or her as a group. They are not counselors, nor do they practice laying on of hands. They, through their commitment to a higher calling, bring the immediacy of a gentle hug and a friendly voice to the worship of God. In far too many places, the structure of ceremony limits personal contact. The individual can feel lost and unimportant in such an atmosphere. The goal of a Healing Helpers Program is to return the art of healing to "the altar of the heart"—to the people who care.

This is what has worked best for the team I started at our church:

• Members of the team walk to the front after services and line up in full view. Anyone needing aid also comes forward. All join hands as a circle is formed.

• The team leader for the day leads the group in a prayer of protection, affirming that each one is centered and whole in God's healing light.

• Team members take turns each week leading the session. The team leader's job is to ask for requests, repeating each person's name and the concern given.

• Prayer is started by the team leader. When the leader is finished praying, he or she squeezes the hand of the person to the left as a signal to that individual to take a turn offering prayer (verbally or silently). Each person in the circle takes a turn in this manner until everyone in the circle has had an opportunity to participate.

• Once all requests are covered, healing prayers are then directed to the needs of the larger community. The session closes with prayer and a group hug. Sessions usually last ten to fifteen minutes.

Miracles are commonplace with Healing Helper Programs. The immediacy of joining hands in personal and sincere caring is a powerful adjunct to the effectiveness of prayer *dedicated to God's will, not our will*— proof positive that at the heart level we are all conduits of the Divine.

How much can we each accomplish as a Healing Helper in our daily lives? Well, here are a couple of stories that may surprise and inspire you.

Nadia McCaffrey, originally from France but now living in California, was one of my subjects in the original research I did with near–death experiencers who had their episode in childhood. She could never quite reconcile with the earth plane afterward and longed deep within herself to hurry a return to "the other side." One evening, while caring for a woman who was dying, she nearly died herself following severe seizures of an unexplainable pain. It wasn't until several days later when she was guided by an inner voice to call me that I learned what had happened to her: Nadia's seizures had begun when our granddaughter Myriam's had, and she had merged with Myriam when she temporarily lost vital signs at the same moment the child had died.

Typical of our granddaughter's unique traits was the demand she made for absolute truth. The child could not abide deceit, pretense, hidden motives, or dishonesty. During the crisis Nadia had another near–death episode, one in which she had to face the truth of what she had denied throughout her life: her mission, the reason and purpose for her existence. When she learned about Myriam and about her special characteristic, she was overcome with both grief and relief. With the two souls linking together, however briefly, Nadia awakened to the extraordinary ways one person can help another. As a result, she has accepted and initiated her life's mission: *to change the face of death* by setting up centers for a new kind of hospice, places where people with special needs can go who cannot afford standard care. She has already been deeded land for this purpose and is actively recruiting volunteers, fundraisers, and professional staff.

Then there's Ellen Louise Kahne of the New York area. Founder of the Reiki Peace Network and Reiki University (Reiki is a type of spiritual healing that directly affects the physical and can be taught), she witnessed the tragedy of the attack on the World Trade Center towers on September 11 from her apartment building some miles away. Although deeply and personally affected, she was troubled by the daily drama at Ground Zero with rescue workers, so much so that she named the following November 24 as a "Day of Healing for All" and arranged with Cross Island YMCA for the space she needed for the project. Her goal was to offer a day of free healing services for rescue workers and their families.

Chiropractors, Reiki masters, spiritual healing practitioners, massage therapists, reflexologists, hospice grief counselors, nutritionists, and experts in several types of bodywork restructuring answered her call, some coming from far away. This collection of healing helpers served over seventy-six people during the course of that day, with one of the massage therapists reporting that he gave between forty to fifty treatments. "One policeman," Kahne noted, "was so drained by the constant work schedule, by the lack of days off, that he needed everything our healing hands could provide. And we gave him everything. At the end of the day he looked happy, relaxed, and at peace, as did his wife and two young children who also received healing. For anyone who was motivated to contribute a donation for our 'free' services, we provided them with envelopes addressed to the September 11 Fund." Kahne has since organized other "Day of Healing for All" marathons and plans to continue them on an ongoing basis as an active force for healing whenever there is need.

We cannot escape our oneness because of variations within life's larger circle of comings and goings. Margaret Matthews understood this when she said: "We have worlds to go, and eternities to do it in." She was at peace, and in her peace she transcended life and death, time and space. What she did, we can all do.

We enter this world on an in-breath. We exit this world on an out-breath. Back and forth. Motion and rest.

16

Prayer's Real Power

"When the heart weeps for what it has lost, the soul laughs for what it has found."—*Sufi Aphorism*

Many times I've mentioned prayer and the power of praying, alone or as a group, but I have yet to explain what I mean when I talk about prayer.

Prayer is *the* most powerful energy in the world, and it is expressed through heartfelt words and feelings. I have witnessed proof of prayer power, with solid evidence, more times than I can count. Prayer heals. Prayer opens the door to miracles, proving that the impossible is possible. I define prayer as concentrated love offered in the name of love. It is the way we have to align our will with the Greater Will, to affirm that the Law of Love works.

Throughout all social groups and in every culture, we are extolled by those we deem holy to pray harder or more unselfishly or with stronger belief so that what we want will be the result of our prayers. We are taught special or secret formulas on how to

∞

use the right words in the right manner. 'Tis the way of the wise, we are told. If we want a miracle, we must humble ourselves in prayer and keep the faith—and this works, usually.

When prayer doesn't work, the reason, we are told, is always the same: it's God's will. The guilt that follows such a decree can be devastating. People blame themselves; they're not good enough, they're a failure, or they don't deserve the fabled blessing.

Check at your local bookstore for the latest scientific findings on prayer in the latest bestseller. They're stunning. Because of that, prayer is now "in." Still, I can't help but notice that there is something missing in the rush to put prayer back in our lives. I would peg this as intention and motive.

Is our intention to be well again, pain free, prosperous, have that perfect mate, make it through the next stop light, find a parking space, win the lotto, be protected and safe, overcome adversity, or simply to say thank you?

There's nothing wrong with any of these intentions. They're all perfectly legitimate. But I submit to you that we can confuse prayer with visualization. Focusing on a desired goal, empowering that desire with concentrated thought, feeling, and specific detail, is how you do a visualization. Athletes can attest to the success of this, and so can millions of others who regularly practice the technique. But prayer, true prayer, is more than a mental exercise.

In prayer we affirm the rightness of things and who's really in charge of our life dramas. Visualization sets the stage for action and gives us tools to write better scripts on how to live, but the technique is too easily sabotaged by ego-override. We can deceive ourselves into thinking something is good for us when really it isn't. Human vision is limited. None of us are as smart as we think. Prayer is like a fail-safe; it keeps us aligned at a level and with a force that transcends human knowing. In prayer, we put the power where it belongs. This is where motive comes in.

My life experiences have shown me that there is but one God, one Family, one Creation, one Law, one Plan. Because of this Truth, I have learned to close my prayers by always affirming: *in accordance with Divine*

Order for the highest good of all concerned.

My emphasis, the motive I choose to identify with, is that of the Higher Good, Divine Order, God's Will; but not in the sense that God is a dictator, because God is not. I have noticed that there is no checklist that God uses to determine who can live and who can't, who can prosper and who can't, who can exist pain free and who cannot. Instead, I have consistently observed that God's goodness is everywhere present and equally so. Literally, there's no place where God is not and no one who is denied access to that Source of Being. God is neither father nor mother; God is love, a kind of love above and beyond human perception or understanding. Even the title "God" is insufficient to describe, address, name, or contain God or the Oneness that is God.

When I relax into this Truth, I become aware of a force greater than anything I know, a presence grander than anything I can imagine, a oneness and "isness" that undergirds and encompasses all things throughout all creation. I encountered the immensity of God's vastness during my three near-death episodes, and still today it is difficult for me to contain my tears and my joy whenever I bring to mind what that was like. Words are useless here. It is enough for me to say that as a result of what happened to me, I now endeavor to put God first in my life. Truth means more to me than whether or not a prayer is successful, for judgment is not mine to make.

A few examples of how I learned to handle prayer power follow:

A number of years ago I attended a three-day conference at a retreat center. Long walks defined the path we had to take from one building to the next. Early in the morning it began to rain—correction, pour. Since the forecast had been for a weekend of sunshine, no one was prepared. I had extra time before class so, using the technique of visualization, I saw, felt, and knew on all levels of my being that the rain would stop and my classmates and I could walk to and fro without incident for the days that remained. Satisfied that I had been of service visualizing this, I readied myself for prayer and meditation. Then it hit me. What would result if I got what I wanted? Comfort, yes, but what about the land? Farm fields and forests were thirsty; a drought loomed.

As I slipped into a prayerful state of mind, I surrendered to God's

∞

greater wisdom. I affirmed my worth as a child of God and rejoiced, knowing that somehow the situation at hand was solved, that all of us were now and would continue to be safe and secure as the waters fulfilled their mission of nourishment throughout the area. I invoked Divine Order, stating that whatever was best for the highest good of all concerned would be what occurred. Then I gave thanks.

No rain fell when I negotiated the pathway. The same was true for everyone else. Once we were all inside the rains began anew. When we had to go outside again, the rain ceased; safely inside, it poured. This stop/start pattern lasted throughout the conference. We remained dry as the land soaked. All benefited. This was a tremendous lesson for me in how the world can work. I did not cause what happened. I chose instead to coparticipate in a grander, better plan; to invoke the Divine.

How I got my name is another example. I was about to marry. At that time in the Commonwealth of Virginia, it was possible to sign a form in advance of the wedding ceremony to legally establish the way you wished your name to appear and be used from then on. Discovering this, I experimented for several days with various combinations, but nothing felt right. In prayer I affirmed that whatever name would be best for my highest good and the highest good of all concerned would soon be revealed to me.

A week later a vision interrupted my sleep. The field of my mind spread with a warm, velvety blackness that shimmered with life. Across its expanse glowed giant block letters that spelled out in brilliant, sparkling white: P.M.H. Atwater. This shocked me awake. I jumped from the bed and landed on my feet in the middle of the bedroom that I was renting from Don and Neddy Repp, a retired couple who lived north of Roanoke. As I stood, I faced a white wall and saw those same block letters suspended in the air near my nose—only this time they shimmered warm black. The colors had reversed. I ran screaming into the hall.

The Repps came running. The three of us talked excitedly about the incident. If indeed this strange name was the answer to my prayer, then it was the silliest ever. I thought the name was brash, egotistical, ridiculous, and I flatly refused to accept it—until I "heard" my complaints. Had I not asked for a name that would align me with the greater good?

∞

Had I not requested heavenly assistance? Back into prayer I went.

At issue was never my wants, but what was right. God knew better than I what would be best for the life I would soon share with my beloved and for my commitment to near-death research. My choice was Truth with a capital "T": nothing less, nothing more, nothing else. By the following week the name felt so comfortable that I couldn't imagine life without it. Considering it a sacred gift, I filled out the proper forms to make it legal. No, the initials do not stand for anything. The name as given is full and complete, and I wear it with joy.

And then there's the one about Myriam.

I wanted Myriam to live; make no mistake about that. Yet I knew that whether she lived or died, she was a perfect child of God, healthy and whole, irrespective of the condition of her body or what happened to it. I absolutely knew this, and I knew better than to plead or wail or demand that her life be spared. Her soul had an agenda to fulfill, an agenda supported by God's indescribable benevolence and love. She was not her body. She was more. As things turned out, Myriam's brain collapsed onto her brain stem. Had she lived, she would have been little more than a vegetable. *Death, in her case, was the healing*, the best possible answer to our prayers.

Myriam's death, though, involved more than the tragic end of a small child.

From her very birth, every time I looked at her I saw Mae. Mae was Louisa Mae Huffman, John's mother, my former mother-in-law, and the great-grandmother of Myriam. She died when Kelly and Natalie were hardly more than toddlers. Kelly was her favorite. Mae had red hair and had always wanted a red-haired grandson. He was the first, a feat that earned him a ten-dollar bill.

I had no problem with the prospect of reentry or who my grandchildren might have been: it was Mae herself. Her eyes looking back at me from Myriam's cherub face seemed strangely intense, like something else was going on here besides a soul returning to the same family it left. There was another agenda, and whatever that was, I knew I must leave it alone. So I said little.

Throughout the waning days of Myriam's life, I was as involved as any grandmother would be. I never allowed myself to consider that she might die. Thought is powerful, so I wanted only positive, supportive, healthy, and loving images of her to fill my mind. When the call came that Friday night and I heard the sob-wracked voice of my son, I swallowed hard. Myriam's fate was sealed. Instinctively, my concern switched to him. My son was in pain, and there was nothing I could say or do to make the pain go away. Gently, I recradled the phone receiver when his voice trailed off and the line clicked.

As I stood in the partially lit room, staring, grief-stricken, Mae manifested right in front of me. I mean physically, although somewhat phantomlike. Caught off guard, I began to cry. She comforted me, filled me with so much love that I trembled. Out of my mouth gushed a flood of regrets before I had a chance to think; one especially of a night when she lay dying of breast cancer and her family stood gathered around her bed, and she asked me if I loved her and I couldn't answer.

John's family was a close-knit bunch who regularly held huge feasts and enjoyed great frolic. Mae had singled me out to smother in gifts, attention, visits, and advice (whether I wanted them or not) in what seemed to me as an act of deliberate aggression. When she died, I felt relief, not sadness, and I refused to attend her funeral. But when I saw how my stance hurt John, I changed my mind and went. Her funeral was one of the largest ever held in the tiny farming community of Filer, Idaho. People flew in from vast distances to pay her homage. I had no idea she had been such an angel to so many, sacrificing even her last dime to help another. I had misunderstood her generous nature, believing instead that she was trying to take over my life. At her funeral, I silently asked for her forgiveness and told her how much I did indeed love her and would miss her.

The busyness of living took me in different directions after that. I didn't expect to see her, and I certainly didn't expect to experience such profound shame stemming from a long-forgotten moment in our shared history. With all the sincerity I could muster, I gave her my love. I felt her pat my cheek, even though she did not move. Then she spoke (I heard her audibly): "Will you write a book about death?" My mouth fell open. I back stepped.

SEEKING INFORMATION ON

holistic health, spirituality, dreams, intuition or ancient civilizations?

Call 1-800-723-1112, visit our Web site, or mail in this postage-paid card for a FREE catalog of books and membership information.

Name: _____

Address: _____

City: _____

State/Province: _____

Postal/Zip Code: _____ Country: _____

Association for Research and Enlightenment, Inc.
215 67th Street
Virginia Beach, VA 23451-2061

For faster service, call 1-800-723-1112.
www.edgarcayce.org

PBIN

BUSINESS REPLY MAIL

FIRST CLASS   PERMIT NO. 2456   VIRGINIA BEACH, VA

POSTAGE WILL BE PAID BY ADDRESSEE

**ASSOCIATION FOR RESEARCH
AND ENLIGHTENMENT INC
215 67TH STREET
VIRGINIA BEACH VA 23451-9819**

∞

All the reasons not to spewed forth. A spate of excellent material now exists from leaders in the field of death and dying and hospice care. What could I say that would make any difference?

She smiled. "You'll be shown. Now, will you write the book?"

I shut my eyes and went immediately into a state of prayer, seeking to contact the Higher Will. A mistake many of us make, I believe, is accepting spiritual experiences and paranormal phenomena either at face value or just because of how we feel about it. We can be deceived when we do this, usually by our own ego. An adage I live by is that wonderful Russian proverb which says: "Trust, but verify." I entered into prayer to do that, to verify, to check on the validity of what I thought I was seeing and hearing and feeling. The rightness of Mae's request was confirmed.

When I opened my eyes, she was still there, waiting. With a deep sigh, I said, "Yes." Mae cocked her head, smiled again, and vanished into the wall. I have not seen her since. What you are now reading is the result of her request.

One day an Episcopal minister came to me and asked if I knew a practical way that he could use to determine what songs should appear in the new hymnal his church was devising. "Sure," I answered. "Prayer."

"No, no, you misunderstand me. I want a practical method I can use to select these songs."

I countered by explaining to him that there was nothing more practical, more real, more available, more dependable to use than the power of prayer. If he trusted his right to ask, he would be led to those songs best for his congregation. He would have a feeling or be shown in a dream or he would suddenly just know. "I depend on prayer," I concluded, "and what results is always what is right."

"I guess I haven't made myself clear," he lamented, then he left.

During my research with child experiencers of near–death states, I was continually surprised by the number of kids who saw the actual prayers being said for them, while they were out of their bodies witnessing what their loved ones were doing. They described how the power of those prayers turned into beams of radiant golden or rainbow light. Seldom did any of them see horizontal stripes of color like a rainbow; rather, they spoke of vertical color bands with brilliant white on either end, as if the beams were long rods or rays. They showed me with gestures how that beam of light arced over from the one saying the prayer, no matter how many miles away, to where they themselves were hovering. The majority of the youngsters who saw this called that light "prayer beams."

Once a prayer beam reached them, some said it felt like a splash of love. Others said it felt warm and tickly. Because they saw prayer as real energy that did real things and had a real effect, these youngsters went on to pray easily and often. Some even sent prayer beams back to God.

In Truth, prayer is not something we do. It's something we are.

Love.

When someone dies, a light goes off. When someone is born, a light goes on. Flickers of the light we possess at the core of our being announce our comings and goings as we enter and leave the bodies and the lives we think we have. It is a wondrous experience during moments of prayer or meditation when, thanks to the inner vision we are all capable of having, we gaze across this vast expanse and see lights, an ocean of them, some glowing steadily, others flashing on or off.

To view the sum of humankind in this manner fills me with a sense of awe, humility, and littleness. The world we live in is so much bigger, fuller, greater than physical appearance would indicate. Our faculties of sight, hearing, smell, taste, feeling, perception, *and* intuition hardly cover what's really there, right in front of us. Science tells us that the average person is aware of only about 10 percent of the electromagnetic spectrum. In simple terms, that means we miss most of what exists.

Instinctively, we all know there's more. We're drawn to religious and spiritual experiences and paranormal phenomena for confirmation of what our gut tells us. With each attempt we make to illuminate that which seems invisible, we expand in our ability to reach other planes of existence and other aspects to what we call life. There's no magic to any of this, just opportunities for discovery. Once we accept the reality of worlds within and beyond our notice, it's almost as if the universe itself rewards us by revealing even more.

17

The Real Truth About Life

"I believe I shall, in some shape or other, always exist; and, with all the inconveniences human life is liable to. I shall not object to a new edition of mine, hoping, however, that the *errata* of the last may be corrected."—*Benjamin Franklin*

For many years after my own deaths and near-death experiences in 1977, I could not attend funerals—out of respect for others. Why? Because I couldn't stop laughing. I'd see the dearly departed standing there, usually by the coffin or near the minister, either enjoying the service or curious about those who were in attendance. After taking it all in, the "invisible" individual would invariably go to the ones who were grieving and lay a hand on their shoulders or whisper in their ear or make fun of them (depending on whether or not there was any rancor present). I deeply understand the pain of loss, but for a while there my first impulse was to applaud, not cry. It's easier now for me to maintain my composure at funerals, but I still smile a lot—mostly to myself.

The dead are alive to me. All the proof I could ever need, I have had.

Of the thousands of sessions I conducted with near-death experiencers, the most oft-repeated phrase they gave was: "Always there is life." These four words require that we ask: If always there is life, how can there be an afterlife? A before life? Life as we think it exists? Perhaps it's not death that we need to redefine, but life!

I know as an absolute truth that every single one of us has a part to play in life's drama. It is important that we play our part with all the heart and soul we can muster. It is no accident that we walk the earth, for earth is God's gift to us—the stage on which we act out our many roles as we change, grow, transform. Actually, the whole universe is our playground. You don't believe me? Perhaps a little science may help to broaden your perspective about *this thing called life*.

Thanks to the Hubble space telescope, galaxies similar to ours with planets orbiting around sister suns have been seen in such abundance that astronomers estimate that there must be fifty billion of them. They reside in a blackness termed "dark matter," a mass of zero-point energy that is heavier than belief and so alive that it shimmers.

Our cosmos is thought to have birthed when a pinpoint of compressed potential was hurtled outward at unimaginable speed. Had this explosion been slightly less violent, the universe's expansion would have been too slow to sustain itself. Had it been slightly more violent, the universe would have dispersed into a thin soup. The ratio of matter and energy to the volume of space at that moment of the" Big Bang" had to have been one-quadrillionth of one percent ideal or creation wouldn't have happened. We wouldn't be here. It's as if the universe consciously desired the life it would one day cradle.

The genesis of stars began in nurseries of towering dust and gas; life as we know it from the waters of a "cook's kitchen," nurtured by experiment after experiment until the right combinations were discovered for producing the forms that through the process of incarnation would enable intelligence to expand. Humans crowned the list, with bodies sculpted as exquisitely as the universe itself. The eminent French scientist Lecomte du Noüy observed: "From the very beginning, life has evolved as if there were a goal to attain, and as if this goal were the advent of the human conscience."

The mapping of our genes, the Genome Project, has proved that all members of the human family are 99.9 percent the same. We no longer need psychics or mystics to tell us we are one. Quite literally, we each are made of the same star dust and breathe the same air; our flesh tones cover the same muscles, bones, and organs—and the same heart.

A spark of spirit fire gives us life, an aliveness fathered by The Source Place of True Essence and mothered by the Breath of God Breathing. We are affected continuously, to some degree by each other's consciousness, for we coexist in the same timeless presence. What is known to one mind is knowable to all minds.

I am amazed at how quickly we lose track of our origins and forget our identity; at how adept we become in substituting what is real for what seems to be real. Cement and steel do not a city make any more than painted planks describe a home. It is a community of minds that builds a city, imprinting every molecule of mortar with the stamp of energy those minds possess and hold dear; and in togetherness grows a home, nurtured by love and blessed by the willingness of those who dwell within to share whatever comes.

We *are* gods in the making, enjoined to take our place with the one great God when we are ready. I have witnessed this while on "the other side"; that's why I believe that the reason we sojourn in the earth plane wearing bodies covered by skin is so that we can explore the urge we have to create and cocreate. We want to see where this flair for creativity takes us and we do that in a process of refinement that seems like school in the way life experiences test us to see what we've learned and what we've forgotten, what we can accomplish and how far we can go. Testing does not happen in the bright worlds of spirit, only where there is the tension of matter, physical matter—the altar where the holy fire is first humbled and then set free.

What draws us to be tested? Flaws. It is clear to me that most of us thrive on challenge and imbalance. It's what perks us up and gets our juices flowing. We seek out the very opportunities where we can learn the most—where we can experiment, stretch, expand, entertain ourselves, take a risk, improve. This is instinct. Tangling with flaws, our own

∞

and those of others, is how we *feel* the life we have.

God does not prevent us from being who we really are. We mostly invent and manufacture our limitations or accept what others would have us believe. On the day when we awaken to the grander reality, it seems as if the world stops, so great can be the surprise of this discovery. The revelations of awakening can be inspired from religious teachings or be triggered by a personal experience that abruptly turns our life upside down while unveiling a powerful spirituality.

Religious teachings, I have found, serve to give us metaphors (symbolic stories) that teach us discernment and understanding, and give us a road map to live by. They offer a communal umbrella of safety and fellowship. When the power of these stories is replaced with rigid dogmas, the empathy we need to honor and respect others, to change and grow, is invalidated. No religious teaching practiced today survives intact from its original source. Only chosen texts and approved interpretations remain for our use.

Personal experiences that deeply affect us, however, are the real change agents in how they shift us from one way of thinking about and doing things to another until *the numinous* catches our attention—life's mysteries. This shift stimulates our spiritual nature and a desire for the intimacy of God's presence as an active component in our lives. Spirituality involves self-discipline, self-responsibility, and the acceptance of self-worth. The practice of spirituality inspires us to choose the higher laws of forgiveness and reconciliation to live by.

Yet, once this truth is realized, whether our approach to life and living is religious or spiritual matters not. Only two religions exist, the religion of love and the religion of fear, and everyone belongs to one or the other, whether one admits it or not.

My experiences have shown me that we are all points of consciousness within the Mind of God. Through the simple acts of being born and dying, we each, as givers of gifts, enrich our earth home and all therein. We give the gift of our potential at birth, what we can become. At death, we leave the gift of our achievement, what we did with what we had.

Two gifts. One we bring in with us. One we leave behind after we're gone. Whether coming or going, we bless this world with the gifts that our existence bestows, the blossoming of our soul.

We are innocents at heart. We all have this little child deep inside whose only desire is to give and receive love, and poke fun. According to my grandson, Aaron, poking fun is absolutely necessary. "People are too serious," he giggles, "so I do what I can to make them laugh." May there always be a child around to remind us of this, what is truly true.

As I was rushing to get the manuscript of this book to my agent, a friend stopped me. "You must read this right away," Harriet Handsfield insisted. Her husband had died not long ago and just recently her niece passed away as well. Shortly before her niece died, she sent Harriet a letter, ostensibly to comfort Harriet, yet sounding exactly as if, at least subconsciously, the niece knew she would be next. She enclosed with her letter a quotation that fit her life, not that of either her uncle or her aunt. "She knew," continued Harriet. "Look at the quotation. It's she, it's my niece speaking through the words, telling me about her own death, preparing me, reassuring me."

The niece was Anne Stuart Hamilton, and she had just finished her very first book before she died (not yet published as of this writing). Here is the quotation she sent to her aunt:

> **Death is nothing at all . . . I have only stepped into the next room. I am I and you are you . . . Whatever we were to each other, that we are still. Call me by my old familiar name; speak to me in the easy way which you always used to. Put no difference in your tone; wear no false air of solemnity or sorrow. Laugh as we always laughed at the little jokes we enjoyed together. Play, smile, think of me. Pray for me. Let my name be ever the household word that it always was. Let it be spoken without effect, without the ghost of a shadow on it. Life means what it ever meant; it is the same as it ever was; there is absolute unbroken continuity. What is this death but a negligible accident? Why should I be out of mind because I am out of sight? I am but waiting for you for an interval . . . somewhere very near . . . just around the corner. All is well."**
> **Henry Scott Holland**
> **Canon of St. Paul's Cathedral, 1847-1918**

∞

The Aramaic word for death translates *not here, present elsewhere.* Think about that, and think about this as well: We coparticipate in our birth and at our death through the energy mass of our soul. This intelligence which seems somehow beyond us, *is us.*

**The only purpose of vision
is to see beyond the view.**

**The only purpose of the
Central Vision is to move the
view. . . beyond.**

Bibliography

After We Die, What Then? George W. Meek. 1987 reissue through Ariel Press, 4255 Trotters Way, #13A, Alpharetta, Ga. 30004.

Evolution Angel, The, Michael Abrams, M.D. Boulder, Colo.; Abundance Media, 2000.

Final Gifts, Maggie Callanan and Patricia Kelley. New York, N.Y.; Simon and Schuster, 1992.

Hello from Heaven, Bill Guggenheim and Judy Guggenheim. New York, N.Y.; Bantam Books, 1996.

Human Destiny, Lecomte du Noüy, Ph.D. New York, N.Y.; Longmans, Green and Co., 1947.

Letting Go, Richard W. Boerstler, Ph.D. Self-published through Associates in Thanatology, 115 Blue Rock Road, South Yarmouth, Mass. 02664.

Miracles in the Storm, Mark H. Macy. New York, N.Y.; New American Library, 2001.

Sacred Contracts, Caroline Myss, Ph.D. New York, N.Y.; Harmony Books, 2001.

Silmarillion, The, J.R.R. Tolkien. Boston, Mass.; Houghton Mifflin Co., 1977.

Sleeping Prophet, The, Jess Stearn. Garden City, N.Y.; Doubleday, 1967 (1966).

Transformed by the Light, Melvin Morse, M.D., with Paul Perry. New York, N.Y.; Ivy Books, 1992.

References

Taylor, S. (2001). *Near-Death Experiences: Discovering and Living in Unity.* (Doctoral dissertation, University of St. Thomas, 2001.) Dissertation Abstracts International (number to be assigned). The fuller version of Scott Taylor's story from chapter 7 can be found here.

Van Lommel, P. (2001). *Near-Death Experience in Survivors of Cardiac Arrest: A Prospective Study in the Netherlands*, pp. 2039–2045. *The Lancet*, Vol. 358, No. 9298, December 15, 2001.

Other Books by P.M.H. Atwater

The work of P.M.H. Atwater, L.H.D., spans a quarter of a century and includes such books as:

The Magical Language of Runes (Santa Fe, N.M.; Bear & Co., 1990)

Goddess Runes (New York, N.Y.; Avon Books, 1996)

Coming Back to Life (New York, N.Y.; Citadel Press, 2001; 1988 reissue)

Beyond the Light (New York, N.Y.; Avon Books, 1994)

Children of the New Millennium (New York, N.Y.; Three Rivers Press, 1999)

Future Memory (Charlottesville, Va.; Hampton Roads Publishing, 1999)

The Complete Idiot's Guide to Near-Death Experiences, with David Morgan (Indianapolis, Ind.; Macmillan/Alpha/Pearson, 2000)

The New Children and Near-Death Experiences (Rochester, Vt.; Inner Traditions, 2003)

Her self-published books are available on her web site at http://www.cinemind.com/atwater. They are: *I Died Three Times in 1977*; *Life Sounds*; *The Frost Diamond*; *Brain Shift/Spirit Shift: A Theoretical Model Using Research on Near-Death States to Explore the Transformation of Consciousness.* (Phase II); *The Challenge of September 11*; *Adults' Near-Death States: A Transformation of Consciousness*; *Children's Near-Death States: New Research, A New Model*; *Subjective Light: Different Types and a New View*; and *A Book of Columns: Another Perspective on the Near-Death Phenomenon.*

For a free copy of her general brochure, send a stamped, self-addressed #10 envelope to her at P.O. Box 7691, Charlottesville, VA 22906–7691.

RESOURCES

Recommended Books—for adults

After Death, Sukie Miller with Suzanne Lipsett. New York, N.Y.; Simon and Schuster, 1997.

After Life, Colin Wilson. St. Paul, Minn.; Llewellyn, 2000.

Afterlife Experiments, The, Gary E. Schwartz, Ph.D., William L. Simon, and Deepak Chopra. New York, N.Y.; Pocket Books, 2002.

Angel of Light, Richard James Cook. Rochester, Mich.; Fountain Publishing, 2001.

Caring for Your Own Dead, Lisa Carlson. Hinesburg, Vt.; Upper Access Publishers, 1987 (continuously updated).

Conscious Universe, The, Dean Radin. San Francisco, Cal.; HarperSanFrancisco, 1997.

Dying Well, Ira Byock. New York, N.Y.; Riverhead Books, 1997.

Facing Death and Finding Hope, Christine Longaker. New York, N.Y.; Doubleday, 1997.

Grace in Dying, Kathleen Dowling Singh. New York, N.Y.; Harper, 1998.

Heart's Code, The, Paul Pearsall, Ph.D. New York, N.Y.; Broadway Books, 1999.

In Lieu of Flowers, Nancy Cobb. New York, N.Y.; Pantheon Books, 2000.

Life After Loss, Raymond A. Moody, Jr., M.D. with Diane Archangel. San Francisco, Cal.; HarperSanFrancisco, 2001.

Next Place, The, Warren Hanson. Minneapolis, Minn.; Waldman House Press, 1997.

On Death and Dying, Elisabeth Kübler-Ross. New York, N.Y.; Macmillan, 1993. (Her web site is http://www.elisabethkublerross.com.)

O Sane and Sacred Death, Louise Ireland-Frey, M.D. Carnelian Bay, Cal.; Blue Dolphin Publishing, 2002.

Return from Heaven, Carol Bowman. New York, N.Y.; HarperCollins, 2001.

Signals, Joel Rothschild. Novato, Cal.; New World Library, 2000.

Still Here, Ram Dass. New York, N.Y.; Riverhead Books, 2000.

Visitations from the Afterlife, Lee Lawson. San Francisco, Cal.; HarperSanFrancisco, 2000.

Recommended Books—for children

Children's Illustrated Encyclopedia of Heaven, The, Anita Ganeri. Boston, Mass.; Element Books, 1999.

I, Monty, Marcus Bach. Honolulu, Hi.; Island Heritage Limited, 1977.

Kids' Book About Death and Dying, The, Eric E. Rofes and the Unit at Fayerweather Street School. Boston, Mass.; Little Brown, 1985.

Little Soul and the Sun, The, Neale Donald Walsch. Charlottesville, Va.; Hampton Roads Publishing, 1998.

What on Earth Do You Do When Someone Dies? Trevor Romain. Minneapolis, Minn.; Free Spirit Publishing, 1999.

What's Heaven? Maria Shriver. New York, N.Y.; Golden Books, 1999.

Recommended Book—for the child in all of us

Children of Light, Jan Royce Conant. Self-published through Stonefield Farm Studio, 23 Three Bridges Road, East Haddam, CT 06423; (860) 434-9030; web site: http://www.stonefieldfarm.com. (Depicts the sparks of Holy Fire coming to earth to experience the power of their choices, then returning to Source much wiser than before.)

Recommended Groups, Projects, Music, and Videos

International Association for Near–Death Studies (IANDS)—This nonprofit membership organization exists to impart knowledge concerning near–death experiences and their implications, to encourage and support research dealing with the experience and related phenomena, and to aid people in starting local groups to explore the subject. They have numerous publications, among them the scholarly *Journal of Near-Death Studies*, a general–interest newsletter *Vital Signs*, and various brochures and materials. Membership is open to anyone; dues are annual and include numerous benefits. Donations to cover operating expenses are always welcome. Audiocassette tapes of IANDS conference speakers are available. Ask for their list of national and international chapters (Friends of IANDS) should you be interested in visiting any of them. Individual reports about near–death episodes are solicited for the archives; to make a report you need to fill out a form, so please ask for one. Memberships, back issues of their publications, and conference tapes can now be ordered directly from their web site at http://www.iands.org/. Also contact them at: IANDS, P. O. Box 502, East Windsor Hill, CT 06028–0502; (860) 644–5216; fax: (860) 644–5759.

Association For Research and Enlightenment, Inc. (Edgar Cayce Legacy)—For safe, practical, fun ways to develop one's intuition, the extensive material, conferences, and training classes offered by the A.R.E. is unparalleled anywhere. Always with an emphasis on spiritual growth and high ethical standards, the A.R.E. is an outgrowth of information obtained through the readings of the late Edgar Cayce, one of the most documented psychics in history. No ordinary psychic, Cayce was deeply religious and committed to the well–being of those who came to him for assistance. This dedication shines throughout everything that came through him in the trance state. The A.R.E. is a membership organization, but its offerings and services are open to the public. Classes in "Practical ESP" (taught by Carol Ann Liaros) and "Intimate ESP" (taught by Henry Reed, Ph.D.), as well as instructional, fun manuals on the subject, are features of A.R.E. programs. For anyone wishing to tackle the psi field and improve his or her intuitive ability (yes, we all have it), what is offered here is highly recommended. Contact: A.R.E., 215 67th Street, Virginia Beach, VA 23451-2061; 1-800-333-4499; fax: (757) 422-6921; web site: http://www.edgarcayce.org. Information packets about its many services are free.

Myriam Renee Huffman Memorial Scholarship Fund (for Returning Students)—Early in the year 2000, a memorial fund was set up at San Jose City College by Kelly and Lydia Huffman to honor the memory of their daughter, Myriam Renee Huffman. This fund specifically targets the returning student who wants to continue his or her education and work toward a degree. Awards are presented twice yearly each time to one male and one female student who meet the following requirements: currently employed in the job field and sincerely desirous of a better life. To apply for this books-and-tuition assistance, the student must write a one-page essay on how the scholarship will benefit him or her. Entries are judged by college officials and the Huffmans, with Kelly and/or Lydia awarding the money. Currently each award is for $500. This will increase as the fund grows. Anyone can contribute via check or money order. All contributions are tax deductible, as San Jose City College is a not-for-profit institution. It is hoped by Kelly and Lydia that what they have done will inspire others across the nation to set up similar scholarships in their own area. There are many opportunities for new students, but not for the returning student who is ready to make an educational commitment. To contribute, send check or money order to: Jane Norris, Student Accounts, San Jose City College, 2100 Moorpark Avenue, San Jose, CA 95128. Be certain with your donation to note that you want the money you give to apply to this particular fund.

Nadia Mccaffrey and "Changing the Face of Death"—As her life's mission, Nadia McCaffrey has taken on the project of setting up centers where people with special needs who cannot afford the care currently available can go for aid—specifically the terminally ill and children with developmental disabilities. Land near Mt. Shasta in California has already been donated to her for this purpose. She is now actively recruiting volunteers, additional donations, and the expertise necessary for construction and staffing. Under the banner "Changing the Face of Death," she gives talks, holds seminars, and teaches classes in how to serve this special segment of society in a way that benefits all involved. Her approach is patterned after "The Final Act of Love" project and her dedication is the same: to provide direct care to individuals and families with special needs while creating opportunities for people of all ages to serve others. Her goal is an all-volunteer organization—no paid staff and no one is ever charged. She also facilitates local meetings of IANDS and has worked with dying patients for many years. Contact: Nadia McCaffrey, 1197 Rusher St., Tracey, CA 95376-2331; (209) 830-9955; e-mail: nadiaiands@aol.com; web site http://www.changingthefaceofdeath.com. For more information about "The Final Act of Love," contact: Elizabeth Calari, 441 Center Street, Boone, NC 28607; (828) 263-8630; e-mail: Ecallari@aol.com. Callari is a certified grief therapist and hospice nurse.

Ellen Louise Kahne and Reiki Peace Network, Inc.—Ellen Louise Kahne is a certified Reiki master/teacher, founder of the Reiki Peace Network and Reiki University, and publisher of *Reiki* magazine and manuals for teaching "Plus Point of Focus" Reiki healing methods. For many years, she has enjoyed an active national and international reputation teaching subtle energy healing workshop intensives in a loving, focused, intuitive, and grounded manner. Her workshops cover all levels of Reiki including teacher training, degree certification, yearly programs in Hawaii, and special classes for children. Her individual sessions utilize vibrational healing, vocal and instrumental sound healing, meditation, breath, visualization techniques, as well as other methods of meeting the needs of her students and clients (even if unspoken). Kahne is also a performance poet and New York liaison for the International Peace Poem Project. Her main focus is to unite healers of all backgrounds, cultures, and healing modalities as equals in service for world peace. Contact: Ellen Louise Kahne, Reiki Peace Network, Inc., P. O. Box 754217, Forest Hills, NY 11375; 1-877-432-5638; e-mail: HealNet@aol.com;

web site http://www.ReikiPeaceNetwork.com.

Unique Video for Personal or Hospice Use—Eliot Rosen has created through his incredible artistry a seventy-minute video entitled *Experiencing the Soul: Before Birth, During Life, After Death.* In documentary style, he interweaves the testimony of people like the Dalai Lama, Ram Dass, Elisabeth Kübler-Ross, and a host of others to present a moving portrait of the human family and love personified. The video is available either by itself or with a companion book by the same name. All royalties go to the nonprofit group, For a World We Choose Foundation. To order, please call 1-888-554-2560. Contact Eliot Rosen at 4892 Petaluma Hill Road, Santa Rosa, CA 95404; (707) 584-7056; fax (707) 584-1088; e-mail: eliotrosen@hotmail.com; web site: http://www.fawwcf.org.

Spiritual/Uplifting Videos for Personal or Hospice Use—I have long promoted the work of Mirtala, a gifted sculptor, author, and poet, because her spiritual insight is unusually deep and rich; in many ways she is in a class by herself. Her story of fleeing Russia with her mother and sister during World War II is a tear-jerker. What she has learned from life and from the perspective of the soul is illumined in the transformative power of her art. I especially recommend the two videos that feature views of her sculptures set to music, as they can be used in any setting without regard to language differences. Videos are: *Mandalas: Vision of Heaven and Earth* and *The Human Journey.* Her e-mail address is: mirtala@earthlink.net.

The Chalice of Repose Project—A unique end-of-life patient care program and graduate level school of music, the Chalice of Repose has been affiliated with St. Patrick Hospital in Missoula, Montana, since 1992. Their vision is to offer unconditionally loving care of the dying through the delivery of prescriptive music. The core of this work is the field of music thanatology developed by Therese Schroeder-Sheker. Music thanatology is a contemplative activity with clinical applications. In contemplative musicianship, Chalice practitioners embrace and cultivate the spiritual dimensions, instrumentally and vocally, required to serve the needs of the dying. They acknowledge that music is far more than repertoire. They understand that artistry and fine-tuning reflect bodily, moral, emotional, and spiritual awarenesses and do not isolate these realities from technical musical developments or skills. Music is understood as a transformative current that bridges and communicates, reorganizes and transforms, binds and loosens. Practitioners, working in teams of two, position themselves and their harps on either side of the dying patient and attentively work with the musical deliveries required to support and facilitate the unbinding process that is central to a conscious, peaceful, or blessed death. To inquire further or to pursue certification, contact the Chalice of Repose Project in care of St. Patrick Hospital, 312 E. Pine Street, Missoula, MT 59802; (406) 329-2810; fax: (406) 329-5614; web site http://www.saintpatrick.org.

Other Music for the Dying—*The Silent Path* by Robert Haig Coxon is exceptional not only for those about to make final passage, but for anyone who wishes to deepen the meditative state or totally relax. The transcendental sound he creates evokes the sacredness of silence and the power of one's own soul. Available on CD or audiocassette tapes, it should be available at your favorite music store. If you cannot locate it, contact: R.H.C. Productions, Box 4172, Westmount, Quebec, Canada H3Z 3B6.

> *Graceful Passages: A Companion for Living and Dying* combines messages and music to open your heart and comfort your soul. More philosophical in content, the material promotes reflections on the meaning of life and death. The double CD gift-book set is the creation of Gary Remal Malkin and Michael Stillwater. To obtain a copy contact: Companion Arts, P.O. Box 2528, Novato, CA 94948-2528; 1-888-242-6608; e-mail: info@gracefulpassages.com; web site http://gracefulpassages.com. If you are interested, request that your name and address be added to their mailing list for announcements of future CDs in their "Wisdom" series.

> *Harness the Healing Power of Music* is the central theme of CDs,

cassettes, videos, and CD–ROMs from Steven Halpern. Request a copy of his catalogue of offerings before making a choice. Anything he does is of exceptional quality. Halpern's music is well known globally for its ability to make a significant difference in people's stress levels, moods, health, creativity, meditation, and spiritual understandings. His work is ideally suited for hospice and hospital settings. Contact: Steven Halpern's Inner Peace Music, P.O. Box 3538, Ashland, OR 97520–0318; 1–800–909–0707; e–mail: management@innerpeacemusic.com; web site: http://www.stevenhalpern.com; office phone (415) 453–9800; fax (415) 485–1312.

Music from the Dawn of Light Programs—Gilles Bedard, an adult near–death experiencer, has developed a unique way of working with music to connect ourselves to our most essential nature. Bedard is a specialist in the field of contemplative music. Although his background is as a journalist, radio program host/producer, and record producer in New Age music (his record label was "Rubicon"), he's been giving workshops on "Music and the New Consciousness" for over fifteen years. He has spent the last ten years researching the psychological/spiritual dimensions of death and dying to develop his program of music for those making the transition. His "Music from the Dawn of Light" is a new approach on the use of music in palliative care. As a complementary resource, he publishes *The Soundworld of a New Consciousness: A Guide of Contemplative Music* and a quarterly newsletter featuring interviews and album reviews. Bedard offers to hospice workers and health–care providers a series of workshops and seminars designed to bring the healing balm of music back into the dying process. Contact him to explore your questions and needs concerning the use of music not only with those about to die, but to enrich and deepen the spiritual component to your own life. Contact him at: Inerson, 9182 Perinault, St–Leonard, Quebec, Canada H1P 2L8; (514) 325–4634; e–mail: inerson@globetrotter.net or inerson@sympatico.ca; web site: http://www.microtec.net/inerson/index2.html.

Compassion in Action—the Twilight Brigade—Originated by near-death experiencer Dannion Brinkley, Compassion in Action (CIA) recruits and trains end-of-life volunteers. These are men and women who spend as much of their time as possible at the bedside of those who are dying, including veterans in the final days of their lives. Their goal is to ensure that "No one need die alone." In the year 2001, the men and women of Compassion in Action volunteered over 40,000 hours at the bedside of both our veterans and civilian population. Supported entirely by donations, this organization operates from centers throughout the nation. For more information, to give a donation, or to sign up for training as a CIA volunteer contact: Compassion in Action, P.O. Box 84013, Los Angeles, CA 90073; (310) 473-1941; fax: (310) 473-1951. National headquarters are located on the campus of West Los Angeles VA Medical Center, 11301 Wilshire Blvd., Bldg. 258, Room 112, Los Angeles, CA 90073.

Wisdom from the Edgar Cayce Readings

Compiled by the editors of A.R.E. Press from the Edgar Cayce Readings CD-ROM

For, it is not all of life just to live, nor all of death to die. For there is no death when the *entity* or the real self is considered; only the change in the consciousness of being able to make application in the sphere of activity in which the entity finds self.   2147-1

First we begin with the fact that God *is;* and that the heavens and the earth, and all nature, declare this. Just as there is the longing within *every* heart for the continuity of life.

What then is life? As it has been given, in Him we live and move and have our being. Then He, God, *is!* Or life in all of its phases, its expressions, is a manifestation of that force or power we call God, or that is called God.

Then life is continuous. For that force, that power which has brought the earth, the universe and all the influences in same into being, is a continuous thing—is a first premise . . .

Then we say, when our loved ones, our heart's desires are taken from us, in what are we to believe?

This we find is only answered in that which has been given as His promise, that God hath not willed that any soul should perish but hath with every temptation, every trial, every disappointment made a way of escape or for correcting same. It is not a way of justification only, as by faith, but a way to know, to realize that in these disappointments, separations, there comes the assurance that He cares!

For to be absent from the body is to be present with that consciousness that we, as an individual, have worshiped as our God! For as we do it unto the least of our brethren, our associates, our acquaintance, our servants day by day, so we do unto our Maker!
                                                                          1567-2

Know that life is a continuous experience, and as there is a consciousness in sleep that is not physical—in the sense of physical awareness—so there is a consciousness in the same manner when the physical is entirely laid aside . . .

Then there should not be sorrow and sadness in those periods when the physical turmoils and strifes of the body are laid aside, for the moment, for the closer walk with Him.

For indeed to be absent from the material body is to be present with the Lord.   1824–1

Yea, pray oft for those who have passed on. This is part of thy consciousness. It is well. For, God is God of the living. Those who have passed through God's other door are oft listening, listening for the voice of those they have loved in the earth. The nearest and dearest thing they have been conscious of in earthly consciousness. And the prayers of others that are still in the earth may ascend to the throne of God, and the angel of each entity stands before the throne to make intercession. Not as a physical throne, no; but that consciousness in which we may be so attuned that we become one with the whole in lending power and strength to each entity for whom ye speak and pray.   3954–1

(Q) Have I any further contact with my late husband, [. . .], since he has passed on?
(A) If that is the desire, it will continue to hang on to same! If it is to be finished, and that which has been to be the development, then leave this aside.

(Q) Does he know of my prayers?
(A) Do you wish him to? Do you wish to call him back to those disturbing forces, or do you wish the self to be poured out for him that he may be happy? Which is it you desire—to satisfy self that you are communicating, or that you are holding him in such a way as to retard? or hast thou *believed* the promise? Leave him in the hands of Him who is the resurrection! Then prepare thyself for same.   1786–2